and Isl

EXISTENTIALISM: A GUIDE
FOR THE PERPLEXED

ON

EXISTENTIALISM: A GUIDE FOR THE PERPLEXED

STEVEN EARNSHAW

continuum

Continuum International Publishing Group
The Tower Building
11 York Road
London SE1 7NX

80 Maiden Lane
Suite 704
New York
NY 10038

British Library Cataloguing-in-Publication Data
A catalogue record for this book is available from the British Library.

ISBN 0 8264 8529 4 (hardback) ISBN 0 8264 8530 8 (paperback)

Library of Congress Cataloging-in-Publication Data
A catalog record for this book is available from the Library of Congress.

Typeset by Servis Filmsetting Ltd, Manchester
Printed and bound in Great Britain by
Cromwell Press Ltd, Trowbridge, Wiltshire

CONTENTS

ACKNOWLEDGEMENTS

I would like to thank all my colleagues in the English Department at Sheffield Hallam University. The students taking the course 'Existentialism and Literature' deserve a lot of credit for making me think so deeply about many of the difficulties which Existentialism brings with it, and are one of the reasons why this book has been written. Danny Broderick and Simon Mullins, who give guest lectures on the course, have been generous in their willingness to share ideas and help broaden my perspective; Colin Feltham, Douglas Burnham, Tony Williams and Jim Sheard have likewise been of great help in talking through queries and interests. Debbie Earnshaw forced me to answer 'What is Existentialism?'

Thanks above all to Liz for her many insights and unfailing support.

CHAPTER 1

INTRODUCTION: WHAT IS EXISTENTIALISM?

Existentialism is a philosophy that takes as its starting point the individual's existence. Everything that it has to say, and everything that it believes can be said of significance – about the world we inhabit, our feelings, thoughts, knowledge, ethics – stems from this central, founding idea. Hence what sets it apart from most other philosophies is that it begins with the 'individual' rather than the 'universal' and so does not aim to arrive at general truths: its insistence on personal insights as the only means to real understanding entails that it makes no claims to objective knowledge. Sartre states that 'being is an individual venture' (1995: 619) and Merleau-Ponty puts it most forcefully when he declares that 'I am the absolute source' (2002: ix). Nor does Existentialism offer a particularly systematic account of its ideas. As a result of this, it is sometimes not classed as a 'philosophy' at all, but something more akin to an association of shared concerns. In addition, there is a certain 'literariness' to Existentialism, so that the prevalence of novels and other literary texts in the canon of Existential literature would seem to remove it further from the possibility of being a philosophy. Many of the 'straight' philosophical essays and books by thinkers such as Kierkegaard and Nietzsche are themselves cast in a literary vein, rather than in the disciplined rhetoric of a rigorous philosophical discourse.

It may well be this focus on individual, subjective truths, its accessibility through literature and its reluctance to define either itself or its areas of interest in any categorical manner, which continue to make Existentialism a fascinating subject. Its concerns are fundamental and immediate to ourselves – who am I? what am I? what life shall I live? how shall I live it? – and by 'adopting' this attitude there is an inherent sense of dynamism, of process, journey, discovery, enlightenment and revelation that is felt and believed to be more important than the building of self-contained, all-encompassing systems more usual to philosophic endeavour. But these questions are framed in Existentialism in a way that makes them somewhat different from the manner in which psychology, moral philosophy, self-help manuals or religion might consider the same questions. We can get nowhere, Heidegger argues, unless we consider the most fundamental of all questions – 'What is the meaning of Being?' – and it is clear, both in Heidegger and in Sartre, that self and existence can have no fixed definition at all: to exist as a human being is precisely to ask the question 'What is Being?' For Heidegger it is a kind of 'potential' and for Sartre it is a 'freedom' 'to be', so that each individual is 'unique' in his or her being and thus escapes categorization at fundamental or universal levels. The most commonly held view of self is that it is an entity which has 'substance' in some way – there is something there, inside of me, which can be located and which I can identify as 'me' or 'I'. However, from Kierkegaard through to Sartre, self is not understood as a concrete entity, a thing that pre-exists my thinking or recognition of it, as if it lies around waiting for me to inspect as the mood takes me. Instead, for Existentialism, self is a 'relational' term, a way of being which dynamically constitutes or constructs the self at the same time as it reflects upon a self which might appear to be already present. For Kierkegaard 'a system of existence cannot be given' (1992: 109 and 118), and for Sartre 'the being of human reality is originally not a substance but a lived relation' (1995: 575). 'Lived relation' alerts us to another feature of Existentialism: the responsibility of the individual to take hold of his or her self in a way which ensures *really* existing, rather than sleepwalking through life. That there are no easy answers to the questions Existentialism raises, and that any conclusions are rare and hard-won, can make the engagement with Existentialism both exciting and frustrating.

The History of Existentialism
Although St Augustine (354–430) and Pascal (1623–62) are often cited as exhibiting Existentialist leanings, the modern origins of Existentialism are usually traced back to the Danish philosopher Søren Kierkegaard (1813–55). There is something misleading in this chronology, however, since Kierkegaard did not really find an

international audience until the beginning of the twentieth century, when he became popular with those later identified with Existentialism: Karl Jaspers, Gabriel Marcel, Franz Kafka, Martin Heidegger, Jean-Paul Sartre and others. Two other writers from the nineteenth century are also regarded as helping to shape Existential thought – Friedrich Nietzsche and Fyodor Dostoevsky – and while Nietzsche came to know the work of Kierkegaard late on, it is unlikely that Dostoevsky was acquainted with it. The chain of influence and development is thus not linear, and it is perhaps anachronistic to call writers and thinkers who were active before Sartre 'Existentialists'. That few of the major writers or thinkers have actually nominated themselves as 'Existentialists' since then is often seen as in keeping with the idea of Existentialism itself, which refuses any attempt to pigeon-hole individuals into prescribed and prescribing systems. In fact, who is, and who is not, an Existentialist, has always been open to argument. David E. Cooper in *Existentialism: A Reconstruction* does not consider literary texts (1999: 12), and also excludes Albert Camus (8–9), who wrote both novels and philosophical treatises. Even more severe would be Jean Wahl's suggestion that only those who called themselves 'Existentialists' should be considered as such, which would limit it to Sartre, Maurice Merleau-Ponty and Simone de Beauvoir (Kern, 1970: 1). Nevertheless, turning to Kierkegaard first allows us to give a historical context to some of the ideas that have come to dominate Existentialism.

Much of Kierkegaard's work was a critique and running commentary on his Christian faith and his relationship with Christianity. The 'aesthetic' works were published under pseudonyms and using *personae*, or voices, through which themes were explored – a fictional or poetic technique rather than a philosophical one. 'What should we choose to do with our lives?' is a central question for Kierkegaard. How can we commit to anything, since any kind of commitment must surely be a leap in the dark? At the same time, to choose one course of action is to close off other possibilities. Kierkegaard also introduced the idea of 'authenticity' and the idea of 'an authentic self' for which we alone are responsible. He described how there was a public pressure to conform to society and that this necessarily led to 'inauthenticity', and that a certain feeling or mood, 'anxiety', indicated or revealed to us that the true nature of our lives is founded on choices which we must make based only

3

on what we as individuals create as values. As such, we are therefore forced to make choices based on 'nothing' that is certain: our existence has no grounding, or, to put it in a more dramatically Existential way, we are suspended over an abyss. 'How to live', 'commitment', 'choice', 'freedom', 'anxiety' and 'authenticity' are key concepts in Kierkegaard and we will see them manifest in later thinkers and writers.

If Kierkegaard is the first 'thinker' in the line of Existential philosophers then Dostoevsky (1821–81) stands out as the first Existentialist novelist. Whereas Kierkegaard wrestled with his Christian faith, struggling from within its boundaries, the works of Dostoevsky, particularly the novels *Crime and Punishment* (1866) and *The Brothers Karamazov* (1880), question the very notion of there being a God, and envisage what a world looks like without him. Without a God there is no given meaning to the world, there are no set moral standards by which we are to abide. But what does that signify? Does it mean we are free to do whatever we want, without moral constraint? Are we free to murder, for instance? Without a God all our rules can be understood as mere conventions – arbitrary decisions we as humans have made, which we can unmake and replace if we so choose. After all, who is there to tell us otherwise? Without a God there is no authority for any particular law or moral, or at least, no authority higher than each individual. Does that then mean individuals are free to set their own moral standards, their own values, become their own gods? Who has the right to say 'Thou shalt not kill'? This is the question at the heart of *Crime and Punishment* when the main character, Raskolnikov, decides to test his individual values against social morality by murdering a malicious pawnbroker; in *The Brothers Karamazov* it leads to the conclusion that 'nothing would be immoral' (Dostoevsky, 2003: 94).

Just as it is not always possible to credit a particular opinion directly to Kierkegaard the writer because he dramatizes issues through narrators and speakers, Nietzsche too sometimes finds it more fruitful to express ideas through other voices rather than speak directly. Nevertheless, we can identify certain themes which Nietzsche worries away at and which inform Existentialism. Again, as with both Kierkegaard and Dostoevsky, the role of God, or his absence, is crucial. For Nietzsche, a godless universe allows each man the possibility of becoming his own God, of living his own life according to self-created values. Not only that, Nietzsche urges that this should be the goal of mankind, or at least a certain type of man within it, who should set himself apart from 'the herd' and follow his own drives and destiny, not slavishly follow those of society. In *Crime and Punishment* Raskolnikov identifies such a man as Napoleon, a genius not bound by social convention. In Nietzsche's terminology it is the *übermensch* (literally the 'overman', although usually translated as 'superman') who should take up this role. Nietzsche called Dostoevsky 'a psychologist with whom I am in agreement', and the influence, or set of similar concerns, is very apparent (Lavrin, 1971: 128).

It may seem strange that for a philosophy so often characterized as atheistic, its origins are so rooted in questions of the individual's relationship with God, or how we might live in a world where God is absent or dead. For later Existentialist writers and thinkers the issue may not arise at all – it is assumed that there is no God, and the matter is of little or no importance. But for those writing in the deeply religious nineteenth century, such as Kierkegaard, Dostoevsky and Nietzsche, the place of mankind and the place of the individual with respect to God underpinned all musings. So even when Nietzsche has Zarathustra declare that 'God is dead' in *Thus Spoke Zarathustra* (1981: 41) there is an intimate relationship with the concept of 'God', and his absence from the universe is of the gravest consequence. Taken together, these religious elements in the origins of Existentialism go some way to explaining why there is a very strong spiritual current that carries through into Existentialist writing well into the twentieth century and why there is often a desire to go beyond the present material, physical being and to achieve some kind of transcendence. Again, however, it should be noted that this move towards transcendence is not present in all writers regarded as Existentialists, and Camus in particular takes issue with any thinking that makes an unwarranted 'leap' from what we know to what lies beyond.

Both Kierkegaard and Nietzsche can be seen as outsiders, in their writings and in their lives, and it is a feature of Existentialism that its precepts and many of its examples present us with alienated figures. The refusal to conform to society's received values is common to both these writers and is a strong thread that runs throughout Existentialism. But alienation – the sense of 'not belonging', of being 'outside' normal society – can be felt in other ways. In Kakfa's *The Trial* (1925), for instance, K. is arrested at the start of the novel for reasons which are never specified. He then finds himself in a world where he is unlike others, forced to defend his existence in a world which comes without a rule-book. Who has charged him? Who are the authorities? Is K. guilty without knowing it? How should he behave? Can he ignore the accusations? Since he is not put in prison, there do not appear to be any consequences to being 'under arrest'. After a series of puzzling episodes whereby K. is no nearer to finding out the truth of his circumstances, someone relates a story to him which has a resonance for the novel as a whole (1978: 235–43). A man comes from the country to seek entrance to the Law. He stands in front of the door but the doorkeeper will not let him in. Behind the door, so he is told, is another door, with a doorkeeper of even more terrifying aspect. Behind that door is another door with another doorkeeper . . . and so on. The man from the country tries everything to get past the first doorkeeper, but fails. Finally, in old age, the man from the country asks what will happen when he dies. The door-keeper tells him the door will be closed – it exists for him only.

The man's search for truth and the granting of meaning appear to lie with some higher authority, which traditionally would have been God, but now in an apparently godless world is uncertain and perhaps impossible. The fact that the door only exists for the man also suggests that meaning and truth are individual matters, that whatever a man discovers is valid for him alone. The closing of the door would also suggest that it is only at the moment of death that the meaning of life can be revealed, although K.'s actual death is very unlike the promise hinted at here. The puzzle of existence, and the necessity to take responsibility for one's existence when there are no guarantees for life other than what each individual creates for his or her self, are both encountered and avoided by K.

If we return to the Existential philosophical lineage, after Nietzsche it is Edmund Husserl's work on phenomenology which leads, quite directly, into the main Existential thought of the twentieth century. His ideas were seized upon by Jaspers, Heidegger and Sartre, among others. He argued that science could only know the world in a certain way which it had already presupposed, but that this was not the way the world was apprehended by individuals. The fact that an object is present or represented in our consciousness has no bearing on the way that that object is in the world. Also crucial for Husserl is that consciousness itself is always 'consciousness of', it is always awareness 'of something'. In Husserl's terminology, such a consciousness is 'intentional' in that it 'intends' the object ('posits' might be a more accessible term). He argued that we should bracket out objects from the world in order to see them or understand them more clearly, understand them without any preconceptions. In this way, and only in this way, could we truly understand 'phenomena' and this would lead us to an understanding of essences, including an understanding of the essence of consciousness.

The most immediate beneficiary of Husserl's thought was his assistant, Martin Heidegger, and it is with Heidegger that the question of 'Being' truly enters into the canon of Existentialist thought with his seminal work, *Being and Time*, published in 1927. Here, 'Being'[1] becomes central to philosophic enquiry, and 'existence' itself is what we need to explore, or, to anticipate Chapter 4, open ourselves up to. Part of Heidegger's argument is that we are all engaged with the question of Being, since only man questions Being at all, and *should* question it. With what has already been said, it can be seen that such an approach has clear affinities with Kierkegaard and Nietzsche, both of whom Heidegger was heavily influenced by. In placing Being alongside time, so that Being can only be understood through time rather than as some abstract, transcendental entity, Heidegger introduces the Existential concept of finitude – each individual's awareness of his or her death. And with Heidegger there is also the awareness of 'others' which demands that we are necessarily in some relation with others, although what this relationship amounts to in Heidegger is open to debate. This putative social aspect of Existentialist thought is often overshadowed by the more self-absorbed subjectivity of Kierkegaard and Nietzsche, and Existentialism, not unsurprisingly, has a reputation for being individualistic and egotistical at the expense of society. This is not entirely true when we look at the detail of Existentialism, particularly with some of the ideas surrounding 'intersubjectivity', for example, in the work of Martin Buber.

If there is one name synonymous with Existentialism, it is Jean-Paul Sartre. It is always wise to treat the Sartre soundbite with some caution, but his claim that '[Existentialism] . . . is intended strictly for technicians and philosophers' (1973: 26) would suggest that he viewed Existentialism as a serious critical endeavour with a cogent set of ideas. Steeped in Husserl's phenomenology and Heidegger's *Being and Time*, his own major work *Being and Nothingness* (1943) is a response to Heidegger's book. It is here that Sartre outlines his concepts of 'bad faith', the 'in-itself' and the 'for-itself'. For Sartre, the self is not a thing which I am and simply refer to when I speak about myself, as if it is an entity with fixed propensities and a personal history which amount to (for me) 'Steven Earnshaw', but is a relation between what is there when I reflect upon who Steven Earnshaw is (the 'in-itself'), and the recognition that in reflecting upon this supposedly fixed thing called 'Steven Earnshaw' I am free to imagine and constitute Steven Earnshaw in a different way (the 'for-itself'). According to Sartre, it is the common goal of human beings to strive for a coincidence of the 'for-itself' with the 'in-itself' since this would remove the gap (abyss) between what I think I find as my self and the fact that I am free to be other than this, and would remove the accompanying angst (anxiety) that this self (being) is based on nothing. I should know that to achieve a state of 'in-itself-for-itself' is a pipe-dream, yet if I refuse to accept responsibility for thus 'making' my self I will lapse into 'bad faith', I will lapse into 'inauthenticity'.

The fifth thinker to be discussed in detail is Camus. Camus, Sartre and de Beauvoir were close friends from 1943 when they met during the German occupation of France, and remained so up until the acrimonious dispute and break between Camus and Sartre in 1952, a major event in French political and cultural affairs. The figure of Meursault in Camus's novel *The Outsider* (1942) has epitomized the alienated Existentialist: he remains true to his own beliefs and emotions, and refuses to accept the dictates and hypocrisy of public morality, even when it means his own execution. In his philosophical essay *The Myth of Sisyphus* (1942) Camus depicts another version of what is taken as a quintessential Existential position: man is alone in the universe, and the only truth open to him is to accept the absurdity of this existence. As with K. in *The Trial*, there is a sense in which we become desensitized to 'existence', we do not take it upon ourselves 'to exist', but merely live a conventional life much as everybody else does; we do not live our own lives. *The Myth of Sisyphus* consequently focuses on another aspect of Existential thought, that to exist is to face the burden of existence, and we should face it with fortitude, we should be aware of it and maintain the struggle with absurdity each day.

The Existential Movement

How much should Existentialism be regarded and perhaps judged as a social movement? It is unusual for a philosophy to attract so directly a following for its ideas from people who would perhaps otherwise have no interest in philosophy. The typical image of an Existentialist as clad all in black, drinking coffee and smoking on the Paris Left bank has endured, though by all accounts the emergence of the stereotypical Existential figure was something of a surprise to de Beauvoir and other Existentialists of the time (MacDonald, 2000: 5). From 1945 to the 1960s was its heyday, as popular versions of it chimed perfectly with increasing individualism and the concomitant anti-establishment attitudes of those decades, particularly with the counter-culture movements of the Beats in the 1950s and the hippy movement of the 1960s, once it had moved outside mainland Europe. Colin Wilson's *The Outsider* (1956) is indicative, offering a popular socio-cultural analysis of the outsider figure in history, but with a major interest in the Existentialists and their ideas, and a bias towards the literary, with Blake and Dostoevsky featuring alongside Nietzsche and Kierkegaard. This populist side of Existentialism probably had little impact on Existential thought 'proper', however, even if it may have coloured later appreciations and criticisms of it. After all, what are now considered the major texts had all been published by 1943 with Sartre's *Being and Nothingness*, or by 1946 if his *Existentialism and Humanism* is included. The social and cultural impacts nevertheless were rather wide, and set in motion a series of books and ideas where other interests are viewed through the concepts of Existentialism, for example: Sociology; Creativity; Education; Theology; Psychotherapy.[2] Some acceptance of existential ideas had quite significant ramifications, for example in R. D. Laing's 'anti-psychiatry' books and practice. A recent book, *Existential Perspectives on Human Issues* (van Deurzen and Arnold-Baker, 2005), would suggest that Existentialism continues to subsist in these related tributaries, a consequence of both the original ideas as propounded in Existential thought and those areas of endeavour caught up in its possible social applications as a practical approach to existence.

The Aesthetics of Existentialism

Although there will no doubt always be a division between those who argue Existentialism should properly be regarded as a philosophy (see below), with any literary and artistic works at best secondary, and those who regard Existentialism as having a wider remit, I think it is fair to say that all those involved have taken a keen interest in the aesthetics of their works, whether art or straight philosophy. Kierkegaard believed that 'the true work of art is "the transubstantiation of experience" and the result of genuinely creative activity' (Grimsley, 1970: 19). He used 'psychological constructions' in order to work through his ideas, a means of engaging the reader on all levels, not just the intellectual (nor just the emotional, for that matter: he had little time for novelists, preferring instead the imagination of 'the poet'). Nietzsche once commented: 'Art and nothing else! Art is the great means of making life possible, the great seducer of life, the great stimulus to life' (Lavrin, 1971: 95). Art therefore has not simply been a pleasant and less demanding tool with which to disseminate and explore ideas; it has been part of the Existential 'concern'. It is not unusual to see arguments suggesting that Heidegger expanded the possibilities of the German language, as perhaps is evidenced by his influence on the poet Paul Celan (Steiner, 2004). Whatever the assessment of him, his attempt to think Existence anew by pushing language to its extremes through his extensive use of puns, etymologies, compound words and phrases, and neologisms, is an aesthetic choice. It is certainly part of the deliberate difficulty of Heidegger in 'unfolding' meaning. Later, Heidegger came to see language as central to how we come to exist and argued that language 'speaks us', rather than a more usual concept of language as a tool which allows us to fully articulate existence. In 'What is Called Thinking?' he states: 'We human beings remain committed to, and within, the being of language, and can never step out of it and look at it from somewhere else' (quoted by Harding in van Deurzen and Arnold-Baker, 2005: 95). On the other hand, Camus deliberately adopts a style that is both simple and 'neutral' (in theory, at least), as if language were a hindrance to the clear, unflinching thought that he espouses. Taken as a whole, the rich texture and density of Existential writing is not an aesthetic affectation; it is part of each philosopher's attempt to render their thinking and experiences in a way which is a proper realization of those ideas, sensations and events. To speak with a 'received language' would be to speak inauthentically. It is natural, then, for each Existential philosopher to create a way of speaking which can be considered unique.

The novel form has been of particular use to the Existentialists, and quite often in the guise of a thriller, literally in works such as *Crime and Punishment*, and metaphysically in a novel like *The Trial*. The reason for this is not hard to fathom. Novels usually depend upon a central character, and throughout the history of the form the focus of the novel has more often than not been the psychological, the inner workings of the mind and consciousness. As such, therefore, it is tailor-made for working through an individual's awakening to the exigencies of existence. The thriller aspect of it is also natural, since the metaphysical is usually a series of questions, most obviously realized in *The Trial*, but novels such as those by Hermann Hesse, although debatably Existential, also follow the metaphysical quest to understand the subjective self. Most spiritual novels have some kind of 'awakening' to the 'true' nature of things, so this in itself does not categorize a particular patterning within Existential narratives, but the awakening of a protagonist's consciousness to an understanding of existence is obviously a central feature of Existential novels (see the section below on 'The Awakening').

I think we might also identify a female Existentialist aesthetic. Virginia Woolf, in a comment on Katherine Mansfield's work, talks of 'moments of being' (cited in Mansfield, 2002: x; the same can be said of Woolf's own work – see below). The feeling of alienation mixed with an overwhelming wonder at the 'thisness' of the world and self is evident in Mansfield's stories 'Bliss' (1918) and 'The Garden Party' (1922) for instance. In 'Bliss' there is the overflowing of a self that cannot be articulated in conventional language or behaviour, and which demands a kind of Nietzschean bodily assertion and satisfaction. Another short story worth considering is Charlotte Perkins Gilman's 'The Yellow Wallpaper' (1892), which has been cast in an Existentialist light (Shaw, 2003). Virginia Woolf's novel *Mrs Dalloway* (1925) suggests a qualified Existential outlook where Clarissa Dalloway is both blessed and cursed with epiphanies, and the sense of alienation and anxiety is ever-present: 'She had a perpetual sense, as she watched the taxicabs, of being out, out, far out to sea and alone; she always had the feeling that it was very, very dangerous to live even one day' (1976: 12). Doris Lessing's *The Golden Notebook* (1962), like the Woolf novel, centres on a female protagonist's struggle to construct or discover a 'self'. She attempts to do this from the fragmented versions of a self that she pours into her colour-coded notebooks. It is 'The Golden Notebook' which represents the ideal self, and as such could fit within the Existentialist scheme of never-to-be-attained 'in-itself-for-itself', although like Sartre at this time, Lessing too is aiming to break out of that pure subjectivity which precludes social and political action.

To class these texts as part of the Existential aesthetic will not meet with everybody's approval, but I would suggest that these women writers are dealing with the same issues as their more cited male counterparts – self, consciousness, freedom, authenticity – even if expressed and executed differently. These issues are not just social ones to do with the changing nature of gender roles in the nineteenth and twentieth centuries, though they are that as well: the notions of 'self' are here every bit to do with 'being'.

Politics

Existentialism might seem a refuge from politics. The focus on the subjective individual would appear to make any consideration of politics and political activity irrelevant. That is not to deny that an Existentialist would dogmatically refuse political engagement, but it would naturally be seen as bound up with the question of Sartrean choice, and thus one choice or possibility among many, singled out according to the individual's personal project. There is certainly nothing in Existential thought itself which necessitates political engagement, although it can certainly be argued, especially in the Sartrean line of thought, that 'to exist' is 'to act', is to be engaged in a manner with the world and others and is therefore not like Kierkegaard's view of existence as a deepening inwardness which has the result of removing the individual from the public realm.

Going beyond this strictly philosophical perspective, matters quickly become complex, and it would be remiss to omit the connections that have been made between some of these thinkers and politics. A direct line is sometimes traced from Nietzsche to the Nazis and the Holocaust, with his idea of the 'overman' and a new elite as a call to arms which underwrites National Socialism. Although Nietzsche's ideas were certainly taken up for this purpose by advocates of National Socialism, it does not really accord with what the reader will find in Nietzsche. Much of the time he promotes the idea of 'the good European' (for example in *The Gay Science* [1882; 1887]) and denigrates all things German. In *Thus Spoke Zarathustra* a passage on 'the State' is adamant that the State is a lie writ large and that only where it ends will we see 'the rainbow and the bridges to the Superman' (1981: 78).

The case with Heidegger is certainly different. He joined the National Socialist Party in 1933, replacing his Jewish teacher Husserl at Freiburg University, and in his inaugural speech he declared support for Hitler's new government. Heidegger never publicly renounced Nazism and he also removed his dedication to Husserl in *Being and Time* in the 1941 reissue. Heidegger's relationships with Hannah Arendt (a Jewish writer and one-time student of his) and Paul Celan (a Jewish poet) have complicated the issue, but most regard his actions and subsequent silence as unforgivable. The question here is to what extent his political views – his support of Hitler and National Socialism – are a result of his philosophical thought. As we shall see, part of Heidegger's philosophy is to view the social world (the 'they') as always leading the individual (the 'existent') into inauthenticity. Such an argument can be construed along Nietzschean lines as being anti-democratic and anti-liberal, but even here it is not clear-cut. Heidegger states that the 'they' should not be seen in negative terms, although it is difficult to see how, given that all the emphasis is placed on being authentic, this can be seen positively. But, in any case, would this in itself inextricably associate Heidegger's philosophical ideas with his political attachments, and then by association would Existentialism likewise be tainted?

I don't think that the first part of the question can be answered adequately, even as it continues to provoke debate. The second part is more easily addressed, since there are a number of Existentialists who actively opposed the Nazis, including Camus and Sartre. Richard Appignanesi in *Introducing Existentialism* (2001) frames Existentialism itself very much within the context of political events leading up to and during the Second World War: 'Camus has chosen an "absurdist" estimate of living at a dangerous time, in 1942, in defeated Paris under Nazi Occupation' (2001: 4) and he quotes Sartre from 1944: ' "Never have we been freer than under the German Occupation . . . This total responsibility in total solitude, wasn't this the revelation of our freedom?" ' (2001: 7). Both quotations identify a connection between the philosophy and the politics, and while Appignanesi says that 'Heidegger cannot be held responsible for betraying a "resistant" Existentialism that he never espoused' (12), he is equally clear that, with respect to Heidegger's silence: 'That right belongs only to survivors of the Holocaust whose life *after it* is unimaginable to us' (152). On the other side, Jürgen Habermas would argue that 'as members of a later generation who cannot know how *we* would have acted under conditions of a political dictatorship, we do well to refrain from moral judgments on actions and omissions from the Nazi era' (1989: 433).

The connection between Existential thought and politics does not end there. It was over political stances that Camus and Sartre fell out, and Sartre is often seen as abandoning Existentialism for socialism. It is Sartre again who articulates the difficulty his brand of intellectual finds when it comes to committing to political activity; it is dramatized in a number of his creative pieces, for example the play *Dirty Hands* (1948), *The Roads to Freedom* novel trilogy (1945–9), and in his essay 'Search for a Method' (1957) which had originally begun as a piece on the situation of Existentialism in the latter half of the 1950s.

Simone de Beauvoir in her novel *The Blood of Others* (1945) explores the relationship between individual authenticity and our being-in-the-world-with-others. The significance of choice and freedom is all the more dramatic for being set among the French Resistance in the Second World War and so the choices facing the individual are political. For de Beauvoir there is the inescapable fact that when we choose for ourselves we choose for others, to the point where we may be responsible for the deaths of others. With her book *The Second Sex* (1949), however, she too began to move away from a more central Existentialist perspective to a primarily political one. In the narrative that puts Sartre and others closely associated with him at the centre of Existentialism, it is indeed politics which brings about the end of that particular driving force.

The Awakening

A common theme in Existential literature is that the protagonist suddenly becomes 'aware' of existence. He (usually) is often shown, up unto this awakening, to have lived an unthinking life, the life of the 'everyday man', as Camus calls him. Kafka's *The Trial* begins with the arrest of K., its central figure. It is an arrest in two senses: literally he is under the constraints of the State, but he is also arrested in the sense of 'brought up short' or 'made aware' of his life, and the reader comes to realize that before this event he was merely living one moment to the next, at work, at play, with no consciousness of his 'self' as self in the world. As soon as he becomes 'conscious', many Existential questions automatically arise: What is the source of meaning in a meaningless universe? How should I live my life when laws and values appear quite arbitrary? Who and what am I responsible to and for? 'But one day the "why" arises and everything begins in that weariness tinged with amazement', is how Camus expresses such an awakening in *The Myth of Sisyphus*

(2000a: 19), and in his novel *The Outsider* this moment occurs when Meursault shoots the Arab on the beach, and his whole universe is torn apart (1981: 64). Kierkegaard argues that 'the only life wasted is the life of one who so lived it, deceived by life's pleasures or its sorrows, that he never became decisively, eternally, conscious of himself as spirit, as self' (2004b: 57). Existential literature often shows this awakening and perhaps encourages it in others, but with the proviso that each individual's awakening is to precisely what self might be, for until there is self-consciousness there is no real or 'authentic' self to speak of.

In Kierkegaard, the awakening of self is signalled by 'anxiety'. When the 'natural man' is in a state of 'innocence' the spirit is 'dreaming', but makes itself known through this vague presentiment, the sense of 'the possibility of possibility'. As the spirit becomes more prominent (or less in its dreaming state) the greater the anxiety:

> Anxiety is a qualification of dreaming spirit, and as such it has its place in psychology. Awake, the difference between myself and my other is posited; sleeping, it is suspended; dreaming, it is an intimated nothing. The actuality of the spirit constantly shows itself as a form that tempts its possibility but disappears as soon as it seeks to grasp for it, and it is a nothing that can only bring anxiety. (1980: 41–2)

This is what we can later term the Existential awakening occasioned by the feeling of angst, the awareness of 'nothingness' upon which the 'possibility of possibility' is dependent. In *The Trial*, K.'s arrest as a form of awakening is very similar to Kierkegaard's idea of the intensification of spirit breaking through from its dream-state.

There is a strong element of 'awakening' in Husserl's conception of phenomenological reduction – the 'bracketing' mentioned above. The process guides the individual into a different attitude to the world, a new way of being in the world that pays attention to the phenomena of consciousness rather than the habitual manner of the 'natural attitude': '*a new way of looking at things* is necessary, one that contrasts *at every point* with the natural attitude of experience and thought' (1969: 43). In Heidegger, the analogous state of awakening is when we become aware of our 'frenetic inertia', the meaningless busyness that we find ourselves involved in every day.

Once alerted to this we feel 'homeless', or, to use the German word, *unheimlich*, literally 'unhomely'. Once in this awakened state, awakened, that is, to the inauthenticity of our lives, we start to seek an authentic existence.

After the Awakening

In Kierkegaard what I here call 'the awakening' occurs when the spirit breaks through from its dream-state; in Kafka the awakening is K.'s arrest; in Heidegger it is a realization of, and astonishment at, the 'isness' of the world; in Sartre's *Nausea* it is the quiddity of the self's world, the 'thisness' breaking through; in Camus's *The Outsider* it is the murder on the beach. For Kierkegaard it is a break with 'innocence' and with the 'aesthetic' and 'ethical' life. With other writers it is a breaking through from the mundane world of habit, of unthinking rituals. But what then after the awakening?

The awakening is accompanied by or initiated by the feeling of anxiety. The concept of 'dread' or 'anxiety', also termed 'angst', first makes its appearance in Kierkegaard's *The Concept of Anxiety* mentioned above. Kierkegaard's notion, which has become familiar in Existentialism, is that when we have, to all intents and purposes, a feeling of 'peace and repose', a state of 'innocence' such as Adam's before the Fall, there is actually always something else there. This 'something else' is 'nothing', and it is this nothingness which breeds anxiety in the individual: 'This is the profound secret of innocence, that it is at the same time anxiety. Dreamily the spirit projects its own actuality, but this actuality is nothing, and innocence always sees this nothing outside itself' (1980: 41). In Existentialism this state of anxiety is usually taken as an 'ontological given', that is, anxiety is a fundamental feature of our existence ('ontology' is discussed below). If the self is a 'potential' rather than an actuality, the self is always a nothing projecting itself forward. This is 'possibility'. Freedom, in Existential terms, following Kierkegaard, is the possibility of possibility. This opens up the world in a dizzying way and induces anxiousness (or we become aware of the anxiety that is already present). It appears to make our selves completely open to the future in an indeterminate way. So freedom, as understood here, completely removes any solid ground on which to base self, since self is merely a projection of its self as it might be. It is not the 'possibility' of self alone which is the cause for anxiety, since this might simply suggest a selection of possible selves laid out before us from which to choose and which in some way would be determinate. It is the very possibility of possibility that causes anxiety.

If many of these thinkers are comparable in proposing some kind of awakening, an awakening to the nature of self and to the nature of the world, the consequent paths they lay out are not always similar. This might be expected, since Existentialism is understood as a recognition of the uniqueness of each self to its self. This is Kierkegaard's point in his book *Fear and Trembling* (1843) about Abraham's willingness to sacrifice his son at God's request – his actions are simply not open to comprehension by others, because his faith is his intimate and unique relationship between his self and God. But it is also a 'leap of faith', what Kierkegaard also calls a 'qualitative leap', by which is meant that it cannot be 'derived', it is not something achieved by logical progression, or by the kind of psychological continuity a 'concrete' self would offer.

It is here we start to talk about 'commitment', not as something I might choose to do once a week, but as a leap of faith which transforms the nature of my existence. And yet how can I commit to something if this means to close off all other possibility? Does that not somehow go against the very notion of 'the possibility of possibility' as something that forms the nature of human existence in general, and my existence in particular? In Kierkegaard this is not ultimately an issue, since the leap of faith is always in the direction the self is tending towards in any case, that is, the movement towards God. That cannot be the case for those Existentialist thinkers who are atheistic. It is here that Nietzsche as a counterpoint to Kierkegaard is significant.

Nietzsche's philosophy is rooted in the body and a will to overcome all physical limitations. This is man 'overcoming' man to become, in a Darwinian transformation, a superior being, a 'superman' or 'overman'. In doing so, in one aspect of Nietzsche's philosophy, this is to accept one's own destiny, which, in the way we are talking here, has some equivalence with Kierkegaard's notion of individual faith, in that this destiny is unique to each individual. How each person recognizes what their destiny is is unclear or, perhaps, like Abraham's faith, not communicable. The 'great man' will know his own destiny, just as the Kierkegaardian man will come to his own faith. Kierkegaard continually stresses the ancient Greek philosophy of 'know yourself', and the same can be seen in Nietzsche. Kierkegaard's 'faith' and Nietzsche's 'destiny' are 'immanent' in each individual, that is, they are part of what constitutes each individual. Since this faith or destiny is known only to each individual as a unique subjective experience, it is not therefore possible to say how people should or might act or be. In Sartre and Heidegger the aim of the awakened self is to take responsibility for the self, to be authentic and live in this potential, unrealized state, rather than slipping into the comfort of the ready-made ideas and habits of the 'they', or slipping into the belief that the self can become a 'true self', as if the matter of self could be settled once and for all. What is required after the awakening is a constant vigilance. Heidegger urges 'resoluteness' and Camus looks to a stoicism or fortitude in the face of the nothingness upon which we try to stand. Sartre often appears more pessimistic, always pointing out the many ways we can fall into 'bad faith' but with little guidance as to what constitutes 'good faith'. Nevertheless, once aware of the 'for-itself', Sartre maintains the idea of 'the project', my life as lived Existentially in a way which only I can be sure of, something which is 'mine' and which I attend to authentically. So while a pattern of 'awakening' can be seen as a constant throughout Existential writing, the fallout from it is quite disparate, although it often involves commitment to a project in one form or other, be this coming closer to God (Kierkegaard), self-overcoming (Nietzsche), living absurdity without appeal (Camus), or being authentic (Heidegger and Sartre).

Finitude

It might be thought that the refusal to define pathways after the awakening is missing the obvious, that we are all going to die. And if that is so, it might appear a little euphemistic to entitle this section 'finitude' rather than 'death'. But the two are not identical, and 'finitude' has a particular meaning within Existential thought, of which death is only part.

By 'finitude' is understood that our lives are finite, they have an end in death. However, as part of our habitual, unthinking mode of existence, we tend to ignore this fact. But for some Existentialist writers, this is part of a general self-deception; they argue that we need to confront our deaths, and only in doing this do we apprehend self and being. It is only through death, for instance, that 'possibility' has any significance in the sense that it entails 'choice'. If we were to live forever, we would not have to bother about making one choice over another, there would be an infinite amount of time to experience all possibilities. That is the premise for the film *Groundhog Day* (1993), where the central character repeatedly relives the same 24 hours, sometimes choosing to be a hero, sometimes a lowlife, sometimes a shallow charmer, until he realizes that to live for eternity removes the significance of choice and therefore meaning. Consequently he attempts to kill himself but because he is trapped in eternity, there is no death – more properly, there is no 'finitude' – no shape to life because there is no end.

'Death' alone does not create meaningfulness, nor exactly does the self's confrontation with its own end. This is because death in the thinking of Heidegger and Sartre is not a future event isolated in time which is yet to happen; it is bound up with the now and how I project myself. Sartre takes issue with Heidegger's notion that we are waiting upon death since, he argues, we can never know the moment of our death. This leads to a greater sense of urgency in Sartre for our lives are the projects we achieve, not the ones we intend to achieve. Camus understands death in a different way. It is the absurdity of life that we exist and that simultaneously death renders everything futile. Why not commit suicide, then? Because that would show that we were certain that life was not worth living, and to be certain we would have to know what the meaning of life is. But to live and pretend that there is meaning, to pretend that death does not make everything futile, is to live a lie. This is Camus's version of finitude.

The Human

In defining 'existence', discussion often focuses on what it is to be 'human'. Are there certain qualities or factors which make us 'human' and which make the 'human race'? The abiding notion within Existentialism is that there is nothing essentially 'human' in the sense of a list of objective criteria which can be said to constitute 'the human'. No thinker would deny that biologically there is something in common which goes some way to defining a 'human race', but for the Existentialist these features can be regarded as relatively trivial. Existentialism understands 'human' to be synonymous with 'self', and 'self' in Existentialism is an uncompleted project, a 'potential' which each individual is solely responsible for 'realizing' or 'unfolding'; 'the human' is not, therefore, something which has a definite material existence in the way an animal is considered to be an entity with describable, fixed features which fully determine the nature of its existence.

This does not mean that Existential thinkers refuse to comment on 'humanity' as a whole. On the contrary, it is usual for them to contrast precisely how the individual is separated from the mass and is obliged to separate him- or herself from it. Further, it is quite usual for this to be placed in the context of the 'age' within which the writers place themselves. These proposed historical contexts have usually been considered negatively. Kierkegaard believed himself to live in an age which had seen a decline in the true meaning of Christianity, and he saw it as his mission – increasingly so in later life – to restore the human race to a central Christian philosophy. For Nietzsche, writing in the second half of the nineteenth century, the human race had become decadent and weak. The descent of Western civilization into decadence was a common sentiment in that period, and his writings proposed how a 'will to power' could prove a counter to this negative attitude. Both Kierkegaard and Nietzsche use a terminology in which 'the human race' is a quantity, such as 'rabble', or to be conceived (in Nietzsche) in animal terms as 'a herd', whereas on the other hand, in both writers, the individual human is a quality, not a quantity.

For some commentators these views might be explained historically as reactions to industrialization, the ever-growing atomization of society into little more than unthinking work-units. Hence it might be that there is a point in common between Kierkegaard and Marx, where each sees the pressure of the age producing people who either lack self-identity amid the city crowd, or, when people are conscious of this, feel 'alienated'. Of course, Kierkegaard's remedy for the ills of the age are somewhat different to Marx's, but nevertheless it is interesting that both identify a sense of 'alienation', however defined. Nor should we forget that after the First World War, and again after the Second World War, the question of what could possibly constitute the human race after these catastrophic events was very much to the fore, and so the Existentialism of Sartre and Camus, and the thinking of Heidegger, can sometimes be seen as responses to these major events.

Nevertheless, we should make a distinction between the kind of argument which presents 'the herd' and 'the they' as the public mass, and ways of talking about what constitutes human being in general. In arguing for human being as a quality in itself, it is claimed by Heidegger that the only creature for whom Being is an issue is the human. A dog does not worry over its being and does not name itself 'dog'; nor does it consciously worry over its future or how it can live its life to its full potential. The philosophical term for the study of Being is 'ontology' and Existentialism, when viewed as a philosophical endeavour, is essentially an ontological analysis (as opposed to, say, 'epistemology', the study of knowledge). Being is not open to scientific analysis – at least, not as we currently understand science. And yet Existentialism, and those writers who have contributed to Existential thought, treat their pronouncements upon human being as if they were giving us 'facts'. That this should be the case relates back to where this Introduction started and from where Existentialism takes its cue, namely, the situated nature of our self, the primary fact that we are 'in the world' and that the world is present to us only through our consciousness and through our 'concern', engagement or passion with our life. From this it follows that what we know of our selves, of our being, cannot be uncovered by scientific analysis. Instead, we understand human being and Being through our own lived experience, by examining our psychology, not psychology as understood in its more modern, scientific mode, but in the older sense where individuals report and reflect upon their own selves and their own perceptions. Therefore, when Kierkegaard devotes a book to the 'Concept of Anxiety' he is arguing that 'anxiety' is an absolutely fundamental feature of our existence, that is, it constitutes our being, it is 'an ontological given' rather than a psychological state which occasionally afflicts us. For physical, natural, human and social sciences, such a conceptualization makes it 'subjective' and thus not open to scientific verification. But for Existentialism the 'subjective' is what is significantly true and thinkers from Kierkegaard to Sartre have been rigorous (in their own terms) in their uncovering of these ontological structures. As to science, and indeed in Kierkegaard's and Sartre's cases, with regards to psychology, Existentialism claims that there are limits to what these disciplines can possibly 'know' or describe. For Existentialists, science is always a 'second-order expression' (Merleau-Ponty, 2002: ix), some considerable way behind the individual's understanding.

Existentialism as a Philosophy

David E. Cooper in *Existentialism* argues that for philosophy 'Existentialism' is best understood as a domain marked out by 'existential phenomenology', so that it would be contained by the thought of Husserl and those who follow in his wake. He claims to have very little time for any understanding of Existentialism outside of philosophy:

> For many philosophers, the word 'existential' is most at home in the expression *existential phenomenology*. There is general agreement that the most significant versions of twentieth-century existentialism are developments, welcome or perverse, from phenomenology, the philosophy elaborated by Edmund Husserl in the early years of the century. (1999: 5)

He is not alone in wanting to keep Existentialism solely within the strictures of philosophy as a discipline. Richard Appignanesi in *Introducing Existentialism* would like to excise all literature with claims to being of the Existential variety, such as Dostoevsky, from philosophy (2001: 14–15). We have already seen that Sartre, while delivering a public lecture on Existentialism, at the same time wanted to claim it for technicians and philosophers alone. On the other hand, philosophy as a discipline has often had scant regard for Existentialism, and Bertrand Russell famously omitted Heidegger (and Husserl) from his *History of Western Philosophy*. Hence Existentialism would appear to fall between two stools, appropriated by many who otherwise have nothing to do with philosophy, while itself wishing to shun these in preference for an embrace from Philosophy proper.

There are a number of things to note. Even where the writers are taking issue with philosophy, as Nietzsche, Kierkegaard, Husserl and Heidegger do, they do it from within philosophy, that is, they are part of ongoing philosophical debates. Although the source of Existentialism is most directly attributed to Kierkegaard, many of the questions Existentialism deals with are those which pertain to the philosophical tradition. Discussions of 'consciousness' often take the Existentialist into the realm of the *cogito* ('I think, therefore I am'), the thinking subject which Descartes argued was the only thing we could be sure of. Husserl takes it as a starting point, for example, and the *cogito* is to be found time and again in Sartre. This line of thought then often refers Existentialists to others who took up the Cartesian challenge, such as Hume, Locke and Berkeley. Even what would seem to be those questions which help identify Existentialism, such as 'What is Being?', can lead the writer (and us) back to the ancient Greeks – 'What is, is' (Parmenides) and 'Man is the measure of all things' (Protagoras) (Appignanesi and Zarate, 2001: 63). That may help to establish a respectable philosophical lineage for philosophy for those who wish it, although of course it does not in itself automatically ensure entry into the domain of philosophy (further complicated by the fact that the parameters of such a domain are open to debate within 'philosophy' itself).

However, the way in which Existentialism is deemed to fall outside philosophy is surely a consequence of the way Existentialism regards itself, for even if it wants to be a philosophy, in its own eyes it cannot be just one philosophy among others: its initial standpoint is that philosophy, as carried through since the time of the ancient Greek philosophers, has missed the point (Heidegger, 1995: 21). More than that, Existentialism is as it is because the thinkers involved in it perceive that there is not only a problem with philosophy itself, but there are also problems with psychology and with the aims of science. It therefore attempts to carve out a way of thinking, a way of being even, or thinking about being/Being, which at the same time corrects these errors and installs itself as a new kind of philosophy. To enter into its way of thinking, it is incumbent on the reader or thinker also to enter into a recognition of what he or she is in terms of self or being – it is not an idea that can be circumscribed and neatly put aside at will. So the problematic status of Existentialism with respect to philosophy is a result of its own content: it is not one philosophy among others; if it is to be accepted then logically it *is* philosophy, but only by calling into question what philosophy is or can be.

An argument against this might be that Existentialism as a philosophy is of the solipsistic variety, that is, that the world is only what I perceive it to be, and hence it is no wonder that the logical conclusion is that Existentialism must therefore be the be all and end all of philosophy. Yet, that Existentialism is not a solipsistic philosophy is clear in both Sartre and Heidegger – we are always 'in the world'. In *Sketch for a Theory of the Emotions*, for example, Sartre writes: '[Consciousness] *knows* itself only in the world' (2004c: 53), and in *Being and Nothingness* he argues that we are only brought to consciousness (of consciousness, of self, of being) through the awareness of others; consciousness is therefore the consequence of intersubjectivity (1995: Part III). Likewise, Heidegger's notion of Being is always to be understood as 'Being-in-the-world', just as in Martin Buber's book, *I and Thou*, to say 'I' is always to bring with it the world of others, the 'I-Thou', and/or the world of objects, the

'I-It'. Indeed, to return to *Sketch for a Theory of the Emotions*, Sartre illustrates the (emotional) response to our seeing a face at a window as one of having our consciousness and body taken over by the other: 'The face outside the window is in immediate relationship with our body; we are living and undergoing its signification; it is with our own flesh that we constitute it, but at the same time it imposes itself, annihilates the distance and enters into us' (2004c: 57). It may be that the one thing that separates the twentieth-century Existential philosophers from their nineteenth-century forebears is not so much the attitude towards God and religion, but that self, consciousness and being are inseparable from the social realm in the works of Sartre and Heidegger; the Other (or others) is part of the structure of consciousness (Sartre) and being (Heidegger); it cannot be hived off as readily as the masses are in Kierkegaard and Nietzsche.

But that still leaves us with the problem of who Existentialism is for. If to be human is to question being, are those people who do not question being somehow not human? In Existential terms they would certainly be considered 'inauthentic'. Does that mean that to be authentic it is necessary to be (or aspire to be) a philosopher and to at least have read *Being and Time* and *Being and Nothingness*? It has always been a joke that *Being and Nothingness* was and is more talked about than read. Its popularity beyond the domain of a strict philosophy is down to notions of self and freedom, notions which easily slip the leash of 'technical' definitions to take on an attractive rebellious gloss. Yet while the understanding of the terms 'self', 'Being'/'being', 'Dasein' and 'consciousness' is itself variable between the Existentialist thinkers and influential thinkers such as Husserl, there is a concerted effort among Existential thinkers to remove anything that resembles the popular idea of the psychological self – mainly that of Freud's 'ego', but also generally any notion of an 'I' that is a solid psychological core – from the Existential understanding of Being and existence. This would then mean that there is an Existentialism proper, perhaps Cooper's 'existential phenomenology' to be precise, which reconceives philosophy and the nature of human being. However, this is perhaps too restrictive since considerations of being and self which likewise reject the popular psychological ego can surely be engaged with outside Existential phenomenology. It is partly why this book also considers literature while aware of the danger of finding

Existentialism lurking in every nook and cranny. The book offers a broader understanding, perhaps, and one which allows more serious consideration of literature as well as philosophy.

Reading Existentialism

The book is divided into two sections: the first devoted to 'Thinkers' and the second to 'Themes' in Existential thought. By 'Thinkers' I mean those key writers I regard as having contributed substantially and originally to the Existential canon. The decision to treat these thinkers separately allows for the differences within Existentialism to be more clearly delineated. In particular, Heidegger and Sartre on closer analysis offer two quite different conceptions of Being/being and self. 'Dasein' – Heidegger's term for human being, for the human existent – is a particular instance of Being in general from which it 'stands out', and while Heidegger details the constitution of Dasein, it is understood as a kind of gift, a particular revelation of Being to human being. Heidegger's ultimate interest is, therefore, the ways in which Dasein reveals Being in general. Sartre, on the other hand, is interested in consciousness, which, for him, is virtually synonymous with (human) being. The key feature of consciousness, for Sartre, is its ability to posit things as nothingness (as opposed to 'perceiving', when we more or less simply receive things in consciousness that are just there in front of us). It is on the basis of this ability to posit via negation (I imagine Pierre who is not present, he is a 'given-absent' to consciousness) that we are free, since we can construct worlds which do not already exist. Hence freedom becomes increasingly important for Sartre in a way that it does not and is not for Heidegger; Sartre's notion of freedom is rooted in a psychological–philosophical understanding of consciousness also without analogy in Heidegger.

For the second section, 'Themes', I have selected certain ideas which are central to Existentialism and discuss both their place within Existential thought and how they are currently regarded. Although Existentialism as a 'social movement' petered out sometime in the 1970s, having begun to forcefully emerge in the 1920s (arguably before) and 1930s, its terminology and ideas remain prevalent in popular culture, in studies of philosophy, studies of literature, in some psychology and psychotherapy, and in the humanities in general. By adopting this approach, I hope to show that Existentialism is not confined solely to the 'history of ideas', but continues to illuminate, at the same time pointing out where its ideas are either incompatible with current thinking, or simply 'unfashionable'.

Beginning to read Existential thought can soon feel like struggling with a foreign language (although the same might be said of other philosophies). This has certainly been my own experience of reading in Existentialism, and when teaching it I start by suggesting it is indeed like learning a new language. Some words are familiar yet have special ('technical') meanings for Existentialism, such as 'anxiety' and 'the absurd', and others are actual foreign words and phrases, such as 'Dasein' and *mauvaise foi*. Understanding in such circumstances demands a frequent looping back, returning to the same idea a number of times as more commentary becomes available.

The advice given above could no doubt be found given to readers just about to take the plunge into any new subject area. But there is something else to say about reading Existential thought and literature which is appropriate to the subject-matter, a demand or request made of the reader by Existentialism itself, which I have already hinted at. The act of reading and understanding is dealt with in Kierkegaard's *Fear and Trembling* where the narrator, Johannes *de silentio*, advises that only by 'labouring' is it truly possible to understand the story of Abraham, and further, that what is missing in the attempt to understand the story is precisely the 'anguish' of Abraham (2003: 58). There are two things here which the narrator is asking the reader to explicitly consider: understanding requires serious effort, and it requires a personal engagement, what Kierkegaard would call 'concern' or 'passion'. Elsewhere Kierkegaard wondered how it might be possible to communicate subjective truth and argued for indirect communication rather than a wholly logical discourse, which partly accounts for the attraction of more artistic philosophic renderings.

What is said of Kierkegaard can be said of engagement with Existentialism as a whole. Although a relatively superficial, popular understanding of Existentialism is readily come by – as a creed that promotes a self that is free to do whatever it pleases, since it exists as its own judge, its own creator, responsible to its self and to no-one else and to nothing else – the literature that composes the body of Existential thought suggests something quite different, something more intense, more difficult, more serious. In *Fear and Trembling*, a work which does indeed place the individual self 'above' the necessity to conform to society's ethics, the narrator imagines a scene where a priest recounts the story of Abraham to his congregation, but without real passion, and a member of the audience, half-asleep, hearing the story and wishing to 'do good' or 'be good' or 'religious', imitates Abraham's actions (2003: 58–9). For the narrator, this 'tragi-comic' scenario is a warning against careless 'interpretation': Existential thinkers do not offer up a philosophy of 'facts' to be learned and executed. Sartre sees the relationship between writer and reader as one that depends upon mutual guarantees of freedom – the greater the mutuality, the greater the freedom, but also in such freedom there is the provocation to greater demands on each (2004e: 41). In the light of which, I hope you will enjoy this book.

NOTES

1 I will use 'Being' (capital 'B') to indicate a more general, abstract notion of existence – for example, trees are part of universal Being. I will use 'being' (lower-case 'b') to indicate when it refers more specifically to human existence, and to when an individual considers his or her own existence. The distinction is far from settled, since what 'Being' is remains contested by the various philosophers. The differences are discussed throughout this book, particularly in Chapter 8, 'being and Self'.

2 For examples, see *Existential Sociology* (Douglas and Johnson, eds, 1977), *Existentialism and Creativity* (Bedford, 1972), *Existentialism and Education* (Kellner, 1958), *An Existentialist Theology* (Macquarrie, 1980), *Existential Pyschotherapy* (Yalom, 1980).

PART ONE

THINKERS

CHAPTER 2

KIERKEGAARD (1813–55)

The philosopher credited with first introducing 'Existential' ideas into the domain of philosophy is Søren Aabye Kierkegaard. His major works appeared in the 1840s and they explicitly argue for a mode of philosophy that begins with the individual's experience of existence rather than the notion that philosophy should work from abstract categories and derive its understanding of existence from these categories. Focusing on the subjective individual, Kierkegaard explores themes which subsequently became central to Existential thought: freedom; authenticity; *angst*; alienation; the individual as 'becoming' rather than 'being'; the self as 'exception'; responsibility for one's self, one's 'existence'; the necessity to 'choose' one's life; the self as a 'relation' rather than a concrete entity; the self as 'style'; the self as 'future-oriented'; the 'leap of faith'; dying as 'mine'. In addition, Kierkegaard's own life appears to offer a model of the Existential individual, absolutely wedded to the 'project' of the self as striving for an authentic existence, albeit within a strictly religious context.

If there is an overarching schema with which to begin to contemplate Kierkegaard's writing, it is with his division of life into three 'existence-spheres' or 'stages': the aesthetic, the ethical and the religious. The relation of the spheres to each other is hierarchical, with the individual striving to move from the aesthetic, where life is typified by the figure of the dandy or seducer, to the ethical, which is best observed in the kind of serious commitment one might make in marriage, and on to the highest stage, the religious. In the move to the religious sphere, as in *Either/Or* (1843), the stage is achieved when the individual personality finally 'chooses itself' or 'receives itself' (1959: 181). In *Concluding Unscientific Postscript to 'Philosophical*

Fragments' (1846) the religious sphere is further divided into Religiousness *A* and Religiousness *B*, where Religiousness *A* is an 'immediate' and 'immanental' relationship with God, whereas Religiousness *B* represents the truly Christian relationship with God, fully aware of the paradox that God, the eternal, appeared 'in time' as Christ, and that each individual embodies this paradox of the eternal and temporal (1992: 555ff.). Although the framework of aesthetic–ethical–religious stages is not one that finds its way into Existential thought, it does most justice to Kierkegaard's body of work to consider it first, and allows a better understanding of those concepts analysed within it which have since come to be regarded as 'Existential'.

The Aesthetic Sphere

The aesthetic is the life of man in his 'natural' state. Kierkegaard's depiction of such a life appears in the section 'In Vino Veritas' ('the truth in wine') in *Stages on Life's Way* (1845), where a number of characters meet to get drunk and, when drunk enough, offer their views in the form of monologues on the topic of 'love', after the format of Plato's *Symposium* (360 BC). The characters show themselves to be solely interested in the demands of living the good life. Similarly, in the first volume of *Either/Or*, we are shown a pleasure-seeker, known as A. He is a connoisseur of all that is sensual and lives the life of a 'seducer'. Neither in the 'In Vino Veritas' section nor in *Either/Or* Volume I is there a sense that the aesthete is troubled by his way of life; there is no question of 'choice' because the aesthete is immersed in his world of pleasure, of immediacy, and remains uninterested in 'the ethical': 'Beneath the sky of the aesthetic everything is light, pleasant and fleeting; when ethics come along everything becomes hard, angular, an unending ennui' (Kierkegaard, 2004a: 305). Yet, as presented in *Either/Or*, there may come a realization on the part of the aesthete that his life is unfulfilled, at which point he will undoubtedly yearn for something else, something other than the life of the aesthete; the enjoyment of one pleasurable experience after another lacks any continuity for the individual and he thus remains psychically disjointed, his personality is fragmented, lacks cohesion. It is at this point that the choice of 'either/or' comes into play, *either* the 'immediate' but ultimately dissatisfying world of the aesthetic, *or* life in the ethical sphere: 'one either has to live aesthetically or one has to live ethically' (1959: 172). The characteristic attitude of the aesthete who, dissatisfied with the aesthetic life and now perhaps aware of the ethical, is one of irony, an attitude that attempts to hold onto the aesthetic life while keeping the ethical at a distance. The aesthete is deluded in this for once he is aware of the ethical realm, there is no choice at all, for to be aware of the ethical and reject it in favour of the aesthetical is to 'sin' (172). But the 'either/or' is also manifest in other ways, and ultimately it might be described as a recognition of a state deep within ourselves which somehow constitutes (or part constitutes) our ethical being, and it is the ethical sphere which is the subject of the second volume of *Either/Or*.

The Ethical Sphere

Volume II of *Either/Or* is in the form of a 'letter' from an older person (B) to the young aesthete (A) of Volume I. B analyses the shortcomings of the aesthetic life, and, while he repeatedly claims he is no philosopher, advises the aesthete how and why he might move from the aesthetic realm into the ethical. In broad terms the ethical sphere is the world of social responsibility, the world of human morality, what Kierkegaard also calls 'the universal'.[1] In this volume the ethical world is typified by the state of 'marriage'. While it is possible to enter into marriage in a purely aesthetic manner, to enter into marriage *seriously* is to commit oneself to the ethical life of things such as duty and obligation. Instead of standing apart from the universal, as the aesthete does, taking his pleasure as and when he chooses, the ethical individual is absolutely bound to the choice he or she makes. The choice has to be 'absolute', otherwise the individual could just as easily 'choose something different the next moment' (1959: 171). 'The aesthetic' is not completely abandoned, however, by the movement to the ethical; it becomes 'transformed' so that the aesthetic of, say, 'first moments' in love, the excitement and thrill at the beginning of a relationship, are embraced or incorporated 'repeatedly' within the ethical.

To take the ethical sphere seriously is in itself to enter into the ethical (170–1), is to move from the aesthetical to the ethical. Being in the ethical sphere is not so much a question of choosing between 'good' or 'evil' as being brought 'up to the point where the choice between the evil and the good acquires significance' (172): 'My either/or does not in the first instance denote the choice between good and evil; it denotes the choice whereby one chooses good *and* evil/or excludes them. Here the question is under what determinants

33

one would contemplate the whole of existence and would himself live' (173). The narrator thereby argues that it is not the actual ethical choices that are made which are important, but the serious engagement with choice itself, with the either/or of our selves. There is a sense in which by taking the either/or seriously, the choices thus made will necessarily be the right ones.

The Religious Sphere

The focus in *Either/Or* is on the movement between the aesthetic and the ethical spheres. The book does not specifically deal with the religious sphere, although there are elements of this. One such passage occurs when B describes the following moment: 'So when all has become still around one, as solemn as a starlit night, when the soul is alone in the whole world, then there appears before one, not a distinguished man, but the eternal Power itself' (1959: 181). In *Either/Or* it is left as just this, as a transcendent moment that is in effect still circumscribed by the ethical. It is in *Fear and Trembling*, published the same year as *Either/Or* (1843), where the moment is more clearly identified as the individual's 'standing before God', and is given its due place within the religious sphere, where 'faith' now replaces the ethical or the universal as a 'higher' consideration.

Fear and Trembling uses the biblical story of Abraham and Isaac (Genesis 22.1–19) in order to explore the nature of faith. In the story God 'tests' Abraham: 'Take your son, your only son Isaac, whom you love, and go to the land of Moriah, and offer him there as a burnt offering upon one of the mountains of which I shall tell you.' Abraham follows God's instructions, but just as Abraham is about to kill Isaac, God tells Abraham to sacrifice a ram instead. The narrator of *Fear and Trembling*, Johannes *de silentio*, seeks to understand the greatness of Abraham within this story. Put simply in a section called 'Attunement' at the beginning of *Fear and Trembling*, the story shows how Abraham 'withstood the test, kept his faith and for the second time received a son against every expectation' (2003: 44).

If Abraham is judged in the ethical sphere – that is, if he is measured against 'universal morality' – he is a murderer (or would-be murderer). His greatness, then, cannot be the result of some wondrous 'human' feat – for example, if Abraham had sacrificed himself to spare Isaac (54), it has to be understood or 'measured' in some other way, on some plane that is not the ethical or universal. Kierkegaard observes how Abraham must have suffered greatly in his faith, and that part of this greatness is that he expects to receive his only son back after the sacrifice *within his lifetime*, even though he knows that this is 'absurd'. There would not have been this greatness in Abraham if he had expected to be reunited with Isaac in the after-life, since that would be understandable in human terms. 'To receive a son against every expectation' demands a faith in God which is really beyond human comprehension, it exists in the relationship between God and the individual alone, almost as if it has a unique language or form each time an individual stands before God. In doing so, since this faith is unique to each individual, and under-standable only within that individual's relationship with God (or at the moment they stand before God), there is 'a paradox, inaccessible to thought' (85), something which is not communicable with others (99), and the individual is therefore 'excluded' from the 'normal' social world: 'the individual now sets himself apart as the particular above the universal' (84). Kierkegaard also puts this in terms of 'inte-riority' and 'exteriority' (96–7). The ethical life demands that the individual's duty is to 'exteriority', that is, the external, social world: 'Whenever the individual shrinks from doing so, whenever he wants to stay inside, or slip back into, the inner determinant of feeling, mood, etc., he commits an offence' (97). 'Interiority', this inwardness, is incommensurable with exteriority, and so interiority again relates to faith as something beyond thought.

Concluding Unscientific Postscript to 'Philosophical Fragments'

Although what has been discussed so far with relation to the different 'stages' or 'existence-spheres' describes in a general fashion the broader aspects of Kierkegaard's framework, it is in *Concluding Unscientific Postscript* that what can be regarded as 'Existential' by later definitions is most fully elaborated.

The book itself is a sequel to *Philosophical Fragments* (1844), in which Kierkegaard addresses a series of related questions, posed on the title page: 'Can a historical point of departure be given for an eternal consciousness; how can such a point of departure be more than historical interest; can an eternal happiness be built on histor-ical knowledge?' The author wrestles with what he regards as the central paradox that Christianity presents: God, who is eternal, made himself present in time. How can it be, then, that the eternal can be temporal; how can it be that God, through Christ, becomes 'historical'? Consequently, how can it be that if man's movement is towards eternal happiness, this takes place 'in time' and has to thus refer itself, again, to something 'historical'? This might seem an unpromising point from which to further discuss Kierkegaard in relation to Existentialism, wrapped up as it is in a rather esoteric point that one would have thought could only be of interest to a Christian theologian. Yet in the sequel, *Concluding Unscientific Postscript* (1846), rather than just elaborate on a few points from *Philosophical Fragments*, Kierkegaard offers a fairly complete version of how he regards the relationship between the existence-spheres, how movement is effected between them, particularly from the ethical to the religious, and how what is central to all this is the 'actual existing individual'. He introduces the categories of 'Religiousness *A*' and 'Religiousness *B*', and in doing so expands upon the notion of the individual's absolute separateness from others the further he proceeds along his way in pursuit of eternal happiness.

Concluding Unscientific Postscript has Johannes Climacus as its author, and Kierkegaard as the book's editor. In the Introduction the editor stresses that the book is 'not about the truth of Christianity but about the individual's relation to Christianity, consequently not about the indifferent individual's systematic eagerness to arrange the truths of Christianity in paragraphs but rather about the concern of the infinitely interested individual with regard to his own relation to such a doctrine' (1992: 15). Following on from *Philosophical Fragments*, the question before Johannes is how he might bring himself into relation with Christianity such that he can work towards achieving the highest good, eternal happiness, which is available to anybody, whether 'a housemaid' or 'a professor' (15), whether intellectual or obtuse.

Climacus begins by contrasting objective and subjective truth, and this is one of the themes that runs throughout the book. Truth is only to be understood as valuable when it is subjective, and by subjective it is meant that the individual takes it upon himself to pursue the matter because he is 'interested', and interested 'passionately' and 'infinitely'. Certainly I could look for the truth in Christian doctrines, and this might afford some kind of objective truth, but this would not be true for me. Objective truths exist outside the individual, and both in regard to Christianity and with regard to philosophy as a whole. Climacus consistently returns to the idea that the only truth that matters is that which is arrived at by 'the actual existing individual'. Preaching of Christianity or the discourse of philosophy are not the truth and cannot provide it in any manner, and the mistake of Christianity and philosophy has been to forget the actual existing individual. Hence Climacus is not concerned with 'knowledge', which can be assumed to be the province of the Church and Philosophy, but with faith, although, as we shall see, this is faith as understood in a very particular way. If ever the individual feels he has knowledge, it is sure that he has lost his way because he will have lost his passion and thus will no longer be subjective; he will have lost a key element to his self as an existing individual because to be certain in knowledge is also to remove choice: 'As soon as subjectivity is taken away, and passion from subjectivity, and infinite interest from passion, there is no decision whatever, whether on this issue or any other. All decision, all essential decision, is rooted in subjectivity' (33). In being subjective, and in moving from the ethical to the religious sphere, Climacus focuses on a deepening 'inwardness' which simultaneously deepens each individual's isolation from other individuals. On the latter point, for instance, the individual cannot appeal to another's subjectivity because to do so would be to move outside himself and towards 'objectivity' (66). The individual in his deepening inwardness becomes increasingly cut off from understanding others and from being understood: 'The course of development of the religious subject has the peculiar quality that the pathway comes into existence for the single individual and closes up behind him' (67). It is also, therefore, a mistake to attempt to communicate directly this subjectivity, this inwardness, for, according to Climacus, communication between individuals is always 'immediate', direct in itself, and even where individuals agree on something, this is not the same as understanding what can only be understood from within the individual himself: 'Suppose, then, that someone wanted to communicate the following conviction: truth is inwardness; objectively there is no truth, but the appropriation is the truth' (77).

In identifying increasing inwardness as the movement towards the religious sphere from the ethical, Climacus also stresses that the individual is in the process of 'becoming':

> Whereas objective thinking is indifferent to the thinking subject and his existence, the subjective thinker as existing is essentially interested in his own thinking, is existing in it. Therefore, his

thinking has another kind of reflection, specifically, that of inwardness, of possession, whereby it belongs to the subject and to no one else. Whereas objective thinking invests everything in the result and assists all humankind to cheat by copying and reeling off the results and answers, subjective thinking invests everything in the process of becoming and omits the result, partly because this belongs to him, since he possesses the way, partly because he as existing is continually in the process of becoming, as is every human being who has not permitted himself to be tricked into becoming objective, into inhumanly becoming specu- lative thought. (1992: 72–3)

Here we can see a number of the key elements of Existentialism: sub- jectivity, possession (what Kierkegaard also calls 'appropriation' and which Heidegger's 'mineness' might be equated with), existence as a process of 'becoming' rather than of a fixed notion of 'being' as essence. It should be noted that Climacus here frames it in terms of objective and subjective thought, and another feature of *Concluding Unscientific Postscript* is that it views subjectivity as operating through consciousness. As much as Climacus talks of deepening inwardness and the movement towards the religious, this is always in part dialectical, that is, proceeds as a kind of inner discourse, without it ever 'lapsing' exclusively into the speculative thought characteristic of philosophy.

The process of becoming is necessarily a perpetual 'striving' after subjective truth. However, striving should not be understood as something that will eventually render us a goal. If we could actually reach a (the) goal this would signify that we had come to 'the end' and therefore would have an overview and be able to understand everything objectively. Coming to the end would in itself be tanta- mount to having a philosophical system. Although we are 'aware' of existence through thought, there can be no identity of 'thinking' and 'being' (an indirect reference to 'I think, therefore I am'; elsewhere in the book Kierkegaard ridicules the notion of a self-identity such as *I-I*, a view which foreshadows Sartre's own dismissal of the possibil- ity of ever achieving the 'in-itself-for-itself'). As soon as I think (the thought) 'I exist', I annul existence, yet in having the thought 'I exist', I am existing: 'It would seem correct to say that there is something that cannot be thought – namely, existing' (1992: 309). Nevertheless, Climacus regards the necessity of 'existing' as a *telos*; that is, the goal of striving, or becoming, is 'to exist', although this can never be fully realized. In other words, 'existence' is not something which just 'is' for me, in the sense that 'here I am, existing', something that I can take for granted and requiring no effort on my part. Existence, in Climacus's understanding, is something that I reach out for, something that I must continually strive for, something that I must, in effect, 'repeat' every day and take responsibility for every day.

Previously in this chapter, the ethical sphere has been regarded as referring to the individual's relation to the 'universal', that is, its dimension has something of 'the public' in it. Here, Climacus distinguishes between morality, which is part of society, the 'world-historical', and ethics, which is strictly individual. For Climacus, the ethical is that existence-state whereby the individual takes responsibility for his existence: 'the requirement of the ethical upon him is to be infinitely interested in existing' (316); 'Ethics focuses upon the individual, and ethically understood it is every individual's task to become a whole human being, just as it is the presupposition of ethics that everyone is born in the state of being able to become that' (346).

The attention paid to 'striving' means that the individual is always 'acting', in the sense of wanting to change things. For Kierkegaard this is something internal; certainly there can be an aesthetic dimension to action, as when somebody conquers a country, for instance, or there may be an external change which suggests something inner, for example if a king becomes a beggar, but action in Kierkegaard's view means acting internally, transforming 'the individual's relation to himself' and to God. The deepening inwardness is partly achieved 'dialectically', through an inner discourse with one's self (although discourse in this sense is not an intellectual debate, it can be the dialectic of 'pathos', something akin to 'feeling', 'emotion' or 'sentiment') so that for Kierkegaard 'thought' can be, in fact is, action. The goal it should be remembered is 'eternal happiness'. Kierkegaard's depiction of the individual's movement as in essence future-oriented is another element which is important to Existentialism, even if the goals towards which the individual moves, as presented by Heidegger and Sartre, are somewhat different.

It is towards the end of *Concluding Unscientific Postscript* that the reader is presented with the categories of Religiousness *A* and Religiousness *B*. Superficially they may seem to have little bearing on what is regarded as Existential thought, but looking at the terms more closely may help to establish some fault lines that will reappear later in this book.

Religiousness *A* is defined as a deepening inwardness in which the individual, with eternal happiness as his goal, experiences God within himself, and finds God everywhere (and thus, simultaneously, nowhere, or rather, nowhere as regards a *specific* relation between the individual and God). The relation is thus one of 'immanence', 'immanental', that is, 'within'. In order to reach eternal happiness, the individual must 'annihilate' his self, because it is precisely his self which is the hindrance to achieving the goal. Such an existence-state is religious, but not Christian, and according to Kierkegaard can exist in pagan cultures. Religiousness *B*, which can only come after Religiousness *A*, represents a 'break' with immanence; it is when the individual puts himself in relation with the paradox, the absurd, that is, with the fact that God became 'historical', the eternal became temporal, through 'the god', Kierkegaard's usual way of expressing Christ's appearance. It is absurd that the eternal can be present in time, but to be truly Christian the individual must move towards this existence-state, and in it, must always hold fast to the paradox, fully aware that the paradox is precisely that which cannot be understood. This relationship would appear to be aesthetic since it involves the external, whereas Religiousness *A* would appear to be solely inward, since it is to do with immanence. Thus it would appear that Religiousness *A* is 'higher' than *B*. However, it is only in Religiousness *B* that I am conscious of being a sinner, whereas in Religiousness *A* my awareness is one of 'guilt'. In Religiousness *A* I retain my identity, I transform myself *within* myself; my guilt is that I know this at the same time as I move towards self-annihilation. In Religiousness *B* I become aware of my situation by a power which is external and which is responsible for my change, and I become a different self altogether in and through the consciousness of sin. In the guilt-consciousness of Religiousness *A*:

> the subject's self-identity is preserved, and guilt-consciousness is a change of the subject within the subject himself. The consciousness of sin, however, is a change of the subject himself, which shows that outside the individual there must be the power that makes clear to him that he has become a person other than he was by coming into existence, that he has become a sinner. This power is the god in time. (1992: 584)

The discussion in this chapter of the movement between the existence-spheres has suggested transformations between one sphere and the next, not forgoing the previous stage altogether, but qualitatively having it within the new sphere. Religiousness *B* represents a complete 'break', a leap proper, which fully embraces or accepts the paradox. For Kierkegaard this is purely in Christian terms, but, I think, it is different versions of such a leap that become important to Existential thought, right up to Sartre's views on commitment and the specific case of his embrace of Marxism (which could be seen as analogous to either A or B), and to Camus's insistence that we accept the absurdity of existence at all times as the basis for an existence in truth. I should point out that not everybody would accept this view of this particular connection between Kierkegaard and the Existential thought that emerges later – we are talking of comparable definitions of 'leap' and 'absurdity' – but that must be left for the reader to decide.

Psychology

The term 'psychology' appears in the titles of many of Kierkegaard's works: *The Concept of Anxiety: A Simple Psychologically Orienting Deliberation on the Dogmatic Issue of Hereditary Sin*; *Repetition: An Essay in Experimental Psychology*; *The Sickness unto Death: A Christian Psychological Exposition for Edification and Awakening by Anti-Climacus*. This is not our 'modern' psychology which operates within a scientific paradigm, using experiments and observations which can be repeated and verified by independent parties. Kierkegaard's usage is what is sometimes called 'phenomenological psychology', dependent upon the observer's report of his or her own mental processes and emotions.

Much of Kierkegaard's writing is taken up with analyses of emotional and mental states, but within his philosophical framework. The titles of his works illustrate this, incorporating as they do 'fear and trembling', 'sickness' and 'anxiety'. As well as these states, which all involve highly subjective apprehensions of self and world, Kierkegaard discusses related states such as 'despair' and 'melancholy'. It is not surprising that Kierkegaard has such an interest in emotional and mental states, since his approach to 'philosophy' is to begin with the individual's experience of existence, and unless one posits a kind of 'amotional' being, that is, someone without emotion, or a purely rational being, it is not possible to separate self from emotional and mental 'states'. As we will see later, this view of the subjective individual as always in a 'state' is both typical and necessary, as we will find in Heidegger's discussion of 'moods' and Sartre's views on consciousness, for example.

It will be noted that these states in Kierkegaard are 'negative' ones – he does not, at least in the first instance, alert us to 'happiness' or 'ecstasy' as categories for serious discussion, although eternal happiness is something we may look forward to – and so it is no surprise that Kierkegaard has a reputation as a 'gloomy' thinker. Ironically, however, these negative states are indications of a self that, if not exactly what we would like to call 'healthy', are essential to good health. They are 'necessary' ailments in the struggle for self-realization, psychological states to be endured, 'suffered', and a sign that the project of the 'self' is under way. Quite often they are 'chosen' by the individual as part of the self's work:

> So then choose despair, for despair itself is a choice; for one can doubt without choosing to, but one cannot despair without choosing. And when a man despairs he chooses again – and what is it he chooses? He chooses himself, not in his immediacy, not as this fortuitous individual, but he chooses himself in his eternal validity. (Kierkegaard, 1959: 215)

In *The Sickness unto Death*, Kierkegaard believes that 'despair' is a sign that humans are above the animals, and awareness of this despair places the Christian above the natural man: 'The possibility of this sickness is man's advantage over the beast; to be aware of this sickness is the Christian's advantage over natural man; to be cured of this sickness is the Christian's blessedness' (2004b: 45). In relating the psychological through, or more precisely as, emotional states and modes of understanding, Kierkegaard implicitly refuses the mind/body distinction, and again this is a feature of the Existentialists, and a natural way of thinking, perhaps, given the emphasis on subjectivity and consciousness as opposed to abstract and speculative philosophical thought.

Authorship, Writing and Teaching
In all of these works Kierkegaard is embarked upon what he terms 'constructing psychologically' (e.g. Kierkegaard, 1992: 494). There are different ways of interpreting the significance of this. It is partly

the fact that the works under discussion here are his 'aesthetic productions', as opposed to the directly Christian works he published
in parallel to these. The aesthetic productions are works of imagination, and the viewpoints are those of the characters that appear in
them: Johannes Climacus, Frater Taciturnus, Johannes de silentio,
etc. They do not necessarily accord with Kierkegaard himself. It is a
literary and imaginative sensibility. Part of the reason for this, as
mentioned in the Introduction, is that Kierkegaard has a particular stance towards teaching. He believes that a reader is brought
to understanding of something indirectly, very much in the maeutic/
Socratic tradition, 'midwifery', where the truth is brought forth from
the individual. This indirect means of communication is part of the
belief, expressed in *Concluding Unscientific Postscript* and elsewhere,
that the inner subjective truth of the actual existing individual
cannot be communicated, it remains within the individual. It is
for this reason also that the works appear under pseudonyms. It is
in 'A First and Last Explanation', at the end of *Concluding
Unscientific Postscript*, that he finally informs the reading public
that he was the author of, in addition to this book, *Either/Or* (Victor
Eremita), *Fear and Trembling* (Johannes *de silentio*), *Repetition*
(Constantin Constantius), *The Concept of Anxiety* (Vigilius
Haufniensis), *Philosophical Fragments* (Johannes Climacus), and
Stages on Life's Way (Hilarius Bookbinder – William Afham, the
Judge, Frater Taciturnus): 'Thus in the pseudonymous books there
is not a single word by me. I have no opinion about them except as
a third party, no knowledge of their meaning except as a reader, not
the remotest private relation to them, since it is impossible to have
that to a doubly reflected communication'; 'In *Either/Or*, I am just
as little, precisely just as little, the editor Victor Eremita as I am
the Seducer or the Judge' (1992: 626). How far we are to take
Kierkegaard at his word is again open to question, but it is easy to
see that there is a logic to using this method if one of the aims is to
present an incommunicable inward deepening, since the body of aesthetic works, taken together and chronologically, replicate this very
movement.

There is one further point to be made, and that is the problem of
language, since, as was noted in the Introduction, Existentialism
develops a terminology all of its own, both through neologisms and
through unusual usage of otherwise common terms, as if evidence that what the language is trying to articulate is beyond being

captured by language. In *Fear and Trembling* we have seen that the difficulties of 'translation' are foregrounded, and this in itself suggests the inherent difficulties of attempting to render what is regarded as beyond usual comprehension (Abraham's actions); in *Concluding Unscientific Postscript* the difficulty of finding a language that can express the unity of finitude and infinitude – the central paradox – is noted, and, more pertinently: 'But what does it take to describe a person in everyday life, provided one does not become hard pressed by the inadequacy of language, because, compared with existing in actuality, language is very abstract' (1992: 465). It is precisely through revealing the structure of the everyday as experienced by Dasein that Heidegger moves towards understanding Being, but done through the recasting of language.

Anti-Philosophy

We have also seen in the Introduction that there is an 'anti-philosophy' strand to Existentialism. Nowhere is this more evident than in Kierkegaard. In *Either/Or*, Volume II, the narrator B constantly claims that he is not a philosopher and in one section attacks philosophy on two grounds. First, it 'turns towards the past, towards the whole enacted history of the world, it shows how the discrete factors are fused in a higher unity, it mediates and mediates' (1959: 174); secondly, philosophers either annul 'contradiction' or 'transcend it every instant in the higher unity which exists for thought' (175). Kierkegaard's objections are that such methods offer no clue as to how the individual, who is always future-oriented, might proceed, and that to 'annul', 'mediate' or 'transcend' contradiction is to misunderstand the irreducible nature of the central, inner tension of 'either/or'. In *Fear and Trembling* the narrator attacks philosophy and those who would attempt to make a system that would encompass all and explain all: 'The present author is no philosopher, he has not understood the System, nor does he know if there really is one, or if it has been completed' (2003: 42–3). Kierkegaard's specific target is Hegel, but he is also making a more general point that philosophy as an activity that seeks to provide absolute comprehension of the world is untenable since it is too distant from the life of the individual, which is both rooted in the everyday and future-oriented: 'I am husband of a wife, I have children; what if in their name I were to ask philosophy what a man has to do in life?' (1959: 176). It is not so much that Kierkegaard is against philosophy as a whole, although this is how the case is presented, as against a particular kind of philosophy whose main proponent is Hegel. Kierkegaard's anti-philosophical stance is one that argues for a different way of thinking, a new kind of engagement, which begins with the individual's reflection upon his or her own existence, and not as an abstract philosophical category, but as something which the individual is right in the midst of. There is something 'relative' about philosophy, since it can only accumulate contemplations and mediations of the past; it lacks 'absolute time' (177) which perhaps is best understood as a failure to engage with the absolute itself (God). It is perfectly right for philosophy to deal with the spheres of 'thought', 'logic' and 'history' but it cannot touch upon the inner individual (178), and in concentrating on the inner necessity or logic of 'history' it fails to acknowledge the freedom of the individual. The danger of writing and language is that it automatically betrays the subjective: 'The relief of speech is that it translates me into the universal' (2003: 137). The incompatibility of an idea which claims truth as an incommunicable subjectivity, but which must be expressed through language and the pre-existing categories that language embodies, is one that can be borne in mind when looking at those thinkers after Kierkegaard.

NOTES

1 It should be noted that 'the ethical' is somewhat differently described in *Concluding Unscientific Postscript*, as discussed later in the chapter.

CHAPTER 3

NIETZSCHE (1844–1900)

Like Kierkegaard, Nietzsche had a great hostility to any notion of a grand philosophical system. But Nietzsche took a different, more extreme route: 'I am not narrow-minded enough for a system, not even for my own system' (Lavrin, 1971: 8). Kierkegaard may have eschewed the kind of all-encompassing system proposed by Hegel and speculative philosophy, but he nevertheless observed an internal consistency of thought in his own writing. Nietzsche, on the other hand, would not have been embarrassed by self-contradiction; for him it was a fact of life, a necessary condition of his way of working as a very particular kind of philosopher, one 'seeking after everything strange and questionable in existence, all that has hitherto been excommunicated by morality' (Nietzsche, 1983: 34). Kierkegaard's use of pseudonymous authors for his major works, what he called his 'aesthetic' productions, was largely so that his readers did not associate the ideas the books contemplated with the personal life of Kierkegaard himself. Although there is some difference between the pseudonym and the author, mainly with respect to the progress each considers he has made towards attaining the ethical or religious spheres, the connection between the author and the pseudonym remains very strong. Even in the first part of *Either/Or*, where A is essentially a 'dandy', an 'aesthete', a 'seducer', there are clearly direct links to be made to Kierkegaard's earlier life, even if he himself may have moved on from this stage. It would not occur to Kierkegaard, for instance, to put his ideas into the mind or mouth of a madman. Yet this is exactly what Nietzsche does in one of his 'voicings'. So whereas we might safely assume that much of what appears in Kierkegaard's work is an attempt to work through, with self-imposed philosophical rigour, certain ideas, using 'irony' and 'dialectics', Nietzsche's mode of writing, when taken as a whole, is closer to unleashing a myriad of competing and conflicting opinions. Where Kierkegaard argues for movement from one sphere to the next, the necessity to do so always motivated by some psychological state such as dread or despair, Nietzsche argues for each man's 'self-conquering' in order that he may achieve some higher purpose, become a 'higher' man. It is with this concept of 'higher man', the 'overman' (*übermensch*), and its associated ideas that we can first approach Nietzsche's contribution to what later became Existentialism. Nietzsche regarded his book *Thus Spoke Zarathustra* (1883–5) as his master work – 'Within my writings my *Zarathustra* stands by itself' (Nietzsche, 1983: 35) – but the books published either side of it, *The Gay Science* (1882) and *Beyond Good and Evil* (1885), also contain ideas pertinent to an understanding of Existentialism.

The 'Overman'

Kierkegaard is very much to do with 'mind' as 'consciousness', and with the self as a dynamic 'relating of self to self'. It is this dynamic relation which forms the basis of each individual's freedom. Although Kierkegaard at times stresses the importance of the balance between the physical, the psychological and the spiritual, there is always a sense that the physical is the subordinate entity. In Nietzsche the emphasis is very much on the 'body' and on 'will', and in this embrace of biological drives we can see the influence of Darwin's *Origin of Species*, published in 1859. Although Nietzsche states his antipathy towards Darwinism (e.g. Nietzsche, 1979: 75), his notion of the 'overman' clearly owes a debt to Darwin's theory of evolution. In *The Gay Science* Nietzsche claims that preservation of the species 'constitutes *the essence* of our species' (1974: 73), although in *Beyond Good and Evil* the significance of the preservation of the species is understood as a symptom of what he calls 'will to power' (2003: 44). The idea of man existing within the framework of the evolution of species is also apparent at the beginning of *Thus Spoke Zarathustra*. Here we are introduced to the wild figure of Zarathustra as he descends from the mountains where he has spent ten years in solitude, and is now come to distribute to the people below the wisdom gained from his self-exile. Immediately we are asked to situate humans on an evolutionary scale, starting a theme that will run throughout this book: 'What is the ape to men?

A laughing-stock or a painful embarrassment. And just so shall man be to the Superman: a laughing-stock or a painful embarrassment' (1981: 41–2). Man is therefore destined, or urged, to 'overcome' himself, to become the 'overman', with as much evolutionary distance between himself and man as man currently has between himself and the ape. But who can do such a thing?

Much of *Thus Spoke Zarathustra* is taken up with describing the struggle of Zarathustra to overcome his own self with all its human weaknesses and physical frailties, and as such Zarathustra not only comes as a prophet and a teacher to the people, but he is also ready to learn more. He separates mankind into two sorts, 'the herd' and those willing to strive towards the overman. The herd is characterized by its unthinking interdependence and its reliance on Christian values. Nietzsche is swingeing in his criticism of Christianity, and argues that the herd's Christian morality has grown out of a situation where the weak have grouped together and produced laws designed to keep 'leaders', would-be overmen, under control, even if there was once a time when these leaders were initially beneficial to the common lot as they helped to establish such communities. He talks of the 'Ultimate Man', which is the stereotypical man in the herd, the man who has failed to take up the challenge of the overman and has 'left the places where living was hard: for one needs warmth' (46).

In moving towards the overman, these exceptional beings must put themselves beyond the herd, outside or above the morals and values of the rabble. In doing so, the overman must forge his own 'good and evil', make his own law tables. It is fine for the herd to continue to exist, as long as it does not interfere with the overman, and, in some ways, as long as it continues to 'serve' him. This aspect of Nietzschean philosophy is not too dissimilar to the arguments for a 'slave society' in ancient Greek thought, and Nietzsche often describes a slave/master duality as fundamental to society in other of his works. There is a precursor of Nietzsche's discussion of the overman in Dostoevsky's *Crime and Punishment*, and, as already mentioned, Nietzsche was certainly familiar with some of Dostoevsky's writing.

In Part Three of *Zarathustra* (out of four parts), Nietzsche develops his idea of the Supermen forming a 'nobility': 'Therefore, O my brothers, is a *new nobility* needed: to oppose all mob-rule and all despotism and to write anew upon new law-tables the

word: "Noble" ' (1981: 220). This too has some echoes of the 'slave
society' schema. By the nobility Nietzsche imagines a race that is
somewhat aristocratic, holding 'noble' values within itself and
within each individual. Since there is no God, the race of nobles is
itself a race of gods. Here we can see that movement towards an idea
that without God individuals might become gods in themselves. It is
certainly how we might read Nietzsche's description of the overman:
'For many noblemen are needed, and noblemen of many kinds, *for
nobility to exist!* Or, as I once said in a parable: "Precisely this is god-
liness, that there are gods but no God!" ' (220). Having removed God
from the cosmos, both here and previously in *The Gay Science*, there
are a number of consequent 'attitudes' which Existentialist philosophy has appropriated and developed.

The 'Will to Power' and 'The Free Spirit'

Zarathustra and other of Nietzsche's writings tend to proceed via
metaphor, aphorisms, poetry, songs and hyperbole as well as discur-
sive argument. This is particularly problematic for the reader trying
to get to the heart of Nietzsche's thought. To take a typical phrase,
what should we make of: 'And he who does not want to die of thirst
among men must learn to drink out of all glasses; and he who wants
to stay clean among men must know how to wash himself even with
dirty water' (Nietzsche, 1981: 164)? Simultaneously it suggests
profundity – we must experience everything, even what is repulsive
and harmful to us – and nonsense – is anybody really going to do
this? how could it pertain to the world we live in? am I really going
to stay healthy washing in dirty water? – yet it is also 'of the spirit'
of the writing, a zest to invert everything, to overturn all received
notions, to break all habits of thought since they might prevent new
thinking, habits which might hinder an 'overcoming' of man by
man. By trying to express something different from traditional
thought, it is as though Nietzsche must find a new way of speaking,
one that does not pay heed to the conventions of (philosophical) language and writing. Readers of Nietzsche undoubtedly find their own
accommodations for his particular style, and should also be wary of
any final pronouncements on what Nietzsche 'means', including
what is written here. The writing style is very much part of the
general Nietzschean project to move beyond the common lot; the
writing exhibits the same passion that it urges in the reader, the call
to arms, to break free of all shackles: religion, society, morals,

comfort, pity, the herd. In doing so, Nietzsche promotes the concept of 'the free spirit'.

This appears very much a positive attitude, and yet it does not have to be so. Nietzsche was not the only thinker in his time to perceive a general meaninglessness to the universe and he had initially been very struck by Schopenhauer's writings from earlier in the nineteenth century and his discussion of 'Will'. However, Schopenhauer's response to a meaningless world had a certain acceptance of the world as is, a criticism Nietzsche also levelled at Buddhism. Nietzsche also took issue with Schopenhauer's notion of 'will to existence' – how can there be a 'will to existence' since we exist as a matter of fact? – and advanced his own 'will to power': ' "He who shot the doctrine of 'will to existence' at truth certainly did not hit the truth: this will – does not exist!" . . . "Only where life is, there is also will: not will to life, but – so I teach you – will to power!" ' (1981: 138). For Nietzsche, 'will to existence' is meaningless, since mankind 'exists' regardless, so 'will to power' is what the reaction or attitude to life should be. It is an assertion of pure will against a universe that has no intrinsic meaning. It is this aspect of Nietzsche's writing that offers an alternative strand to Kierkegaard's theistic understanding. In the Existentialist line, the overman aspect of Nietzsche's writing leads the way to a more practical incitement, or, rather, it is the desire not to be bound by convention mixed with a will that places the self in a position where it is continuously over-reaching itself as action within the world. However, we can see that there is nevertheless a parallel between the forward projection of the Kierkegaardian self and the forward projection of the Nietzschean self. Both posit a realization of the self as something the self is always heading towards – Kierkegaard by way of giving the self over to God and receiving it back, and Nietzsche by way of accepting the self's destiny, its bundle of drives. Both see any 'current' or 'immediate' self as incomplete, or, to anticipate Sartre, as a self that is not its self.

For Nietzsche it is the 'free spirit' who accepts the fundamental human drive of 'will to power'. In *The Gay Science* he writes:

Once a human being reaches the fundamental conviction that he *must* be commanded, he becomes 'a believer.' Conversely, one could conceive of such a pleasure and power of self-determination, such a *freedom* of the will that the spirit would take leave of all faith and every wish for certainty, being practiced in maintaining himself on insubstantial ropes and possibilities and dancing even near abysses. Such a spirit would be the *free spirit* par excellence. (1974: 289–90)

This should not be confused with 'free will', for as Nietzsche notes in *Beyond Good and Evil*, it is a redundant phrase: to say 'unfree will' is nonsense (2003: 50).

Truth, Self and Knowledge

What should we understand about 'good' and 'evil', about morality, in Nietzsche's thinking? Again, the attitude or philosophy is a consequence of the death of God. In a universe that is believed to be overseen by God (or a god), all meaning and morality are derived from that source, present to human beings either through direct contact with God (revelation, contemplation), through intermediaries (for example priests), or through holy writings (the Bible). Take God away and where do meaning and morality come from? Without a religious framework, should we even be talking in terms of 'good' and 'evil'?

In Nietzsche's view, the overman is beyond good and evil. More strictly speaking, it is for the overman to create his own values; 'good' and 'evil' have no meaning for the overman since they are mere conventions by which the rabble lives its life. For Nietzsche, the people have created 'God', invested him with the values they desire and which they then follow as if these values had been decreed by divine will. All peoples and all states do this, and so, even as a state or a people can proclaim the universality of their worlds, Nietzsche shows their morality and truth to be relative, since different peoples and states have conflicting notions of 'good' and 'evil': 'I offer you this sign: every people speaks its own language of good and evil: its neighbour does not understand this language. It invented this language for itself in custom and law' (1981: 76). There is nothing innate about good and evil, therefore; what counts as 'good' and what counts as 'evil' are culturally relative, and between states and peoples might be reversed. In *Beyond Good and Evil* morality, the ordering of 'good' and 'evil', emerges from what the herd wants. Thus the utilitarian idea of the greatest good holds sway at the time Nietzsche writes, and anything that is outside of this is regarded as 'evil': 'How much or how little that is dangerous to the community, dangerous to equality, resides in an opinion, in a condition or emotion, in a will, in a talent, that is now the moral perspective: here again fear is the mother of morality' (2003: 123). The herd as a grouping, which might be 'family groups, communities, tribes, nations, states, churches' (120) creates a 'form', a container that must be filled with its morality. Against this herd dominance, the 'commander' ('master') figure has declined, and, as in *Crime and Punishment*, it is Napoleon who is recognized as the last of this type of figure. For Nietzsche, over and against the herd, therefore, individuals are free to create their own system of values, since there are none that can be said to be pre-given or universal.

The idea that individuals can (and should) devise and live by their own rules and values has been a very strong idea within Existentialist thought. It accords with Kierkegaard's invitation to the individual to be like Abraham and make authentic choices regardless of what society says. It is the struggle that Raskolnikov faces in *Crime and Punishment*. But if each individual is to make his or her own values, what happens to the concept of 'truth', once the holy grail of philosophy. In Nietzsche's view, as with 'good' and 'evil', what counts as true in the universal world is purely dependent on vested interests and cannot be regarded as objective. In *The Gay Science* knowledge itself is simply a way of making the strange familiar, and as for 'truth', it is not even a question of subject versus object, or 'the thing in itself' versus representation. Nietzsche goes as far as to say that 'We simply lack any organ for knowledge, for "truth": we "know" (or believe or imagine) just as much as may be *useful* in the interests of the human herd, the species; and even what is here called "utility" is ultimately also a mere belief, something imaginary' (1974: 300). In *Beyond Good and Evil* Nietzsche first attacks a fundamental precept of philosophy that 'will to truth' is a good in itself, and perhaps the highest good. Nietzsche asserts that there is something even more fundamental behind this – again, species preservation, affirmation of life, and that, if this is the case, 'untruth' is just as much a part of this will as 'truth' is. Thus philosophers, while they may claim that they are seekers after universal 'truth', are doing nothing more than justifying their own opinions: 'cunning pleaders for their prejudices, which they baptize "truths"' (2003: 36). Instead of looking at any philosopher's particular truth we should work backwards and first ask 'what morality does this (does *he* –) aim at?' (37). Whereas Kierkegaard argued against philosophy on the grounds that as soon as it aspired to objectivity, its very 'disinterestedness' meant that it could not speak to the life of the 'actual existing individual', Nietzsche attacks philosophy because it is mistaken in the first place if it thinks philosophers can escape their subjectivity in any way, that is, they cannot avoid but be 'interested', cannot avoid being guided by what their passions (drives) are: '[Philosophy] always creates the world in its own image, it cannot do otherwise; philosophy is this tyrannical drive itself, the most spiritual will to power, to "creation of the world", to *causa prima*' (39). In both Kierkegaard and Nietzsche, therefore, it is the 'subjective' that is fundamental for any activity that might want to regard itself as philosophy and to which the philosopher needs to attend. When Nietzsche proclaims in *Beyond Good and Evil* that 'A thing explained is a thing we have no further concern with. – What did that god mean who counselled: "know thyself!"'? Does that perhaps mean: "Have no further concern with thyself! become objective!" ' (92), he is in agreement with Kierkegaard's attack on 'objective knowledge'.

Having come this far, it might be reasonable to suppose that the Cartesian *cogito* – 'I think, therefore I am' – would provide a basis for philosophy, since this allows the individual subject to have this certainty if no other. However, Nietzsche takes issue with this as well, since it makes a number of unjustifiable assumptions:

> when I analyse the event expressed in the sentence 'I think', I acquire a series of rash assertions which are difficult, perhaps impossible, to prove – for example, that it is *I* who think, that it has to be something at all which thinks, that thinking is an activity and operation on the part of an entity thought of as a cause, that an 'I' exists, finally that what is designated by 'thinking' has already been determined – that I *know* what thinking is. For if I had not already decided that matter within myself, by what standard could I determine that what is happening is not perhaps 'willing' or 'feeling'? Enough: this 'I think' presupposes that I *compare* my present state with other known states of myself in order to determine what it is: on account of this retrospective connection with other 'knowledge' at any rate it possesses no immediate certainty for me. (2003: 46)

When philosophy puts 'I think' as the secure base from which to venture out into seeking further knowledge, Nietzsche suggests that it presumes too much, for how are we to know that this is 'thinking'? It could just as easily be 'willing' or 'feeling' – there can thus be no self-identity in thought which would therefore allow a self-knowing. But even further, Nietzsche questions the 'I'. What is this 'I'? The 'I think' suggests that an 'I' brings a thought into being, wills it. Nietzsche argues that this is not the case at all, that it is more the case that 'thinking' happens – 'a thought comes when "it" wants, not when "I" want' (47) – that the 'I' is merely a reference point or a necessity of grammar; 'it thinks' would be closer to the mark, but even there at some stage we should really remove the 'it'. There is another misapprehension as well if we conceive of our activity in terms of 'will', for 'will' is nothing but a convenient term for a whole collection of physiological drives.

Nietzsche does not abandon truth, self and knowledge; he is reconfiguring the terms in which they might be understood. Once he has done this, in *Beyond Good and Evil*, he talks about the need for the free spirit to embark upon a dangerous journey, to explore the deepest, darkest and worst recesses of the self. This is the task for the new kind of philosopher, for a new kind of psychologist, one who will accept that in the 'economy of life' 'the emotions of hatred, envy, covetousness, and lust for domination' should be considered 'as life-conditioning emotions' every bit as much as those emotions usually regarded in a more positive light (53). This will lead to 'dangerous knowledge'. As Kierkegaard urges the individual to greater inwardness and to transformations of self which are irreversible, Nietzsche urges the individual to remove all received ideas that are a barrier to greater understanding, something that will lead to understandings from which there is no return. There are also parallels between Kierkegaard's depiction of the test of Abraham, as a test of individual strength, and Nietzsche's vision of the free spirit:

> One must test oneself to see whether one is destined for independence and command; and one must do so at the proper time. One should not avoid one's tests, although they are perhaps the most dangerous game one could play and are in the end tests which are taken before ourselves and before no other judge. (2003: 70)

Of course, for Kierkegaard God is the judge, although it could be argued that it is the individual himself who brings himself to this point, but in Nietzsche's godless universe it is the new philosopher, the new psychologist, the 'free spirit' who must have the courage to wrestle continuously with his or her self.

Authenticity

In *The Gay Science* we see in Nietzsche's terms how the self should strive to be authentic. In section 270, Nietzsche asks: '*What does your conscience say?* – "You shall become the person you are."' [1] The individual is encouraged to be authentic (have a 'good conscience') by journeying towards the true self, just as Kierkegaard, in a religious setting, urges the individual to achieve self-actualization through the movement towards God (in both cases, the present 'self' is not the 'real self' or fully realized self – a point upon which Existentialist thought is quite consistent. A consequence of this for Nietzsche appears in an interesting aside, that 'you are always a different person' (1974: 246). However, Nietzsche also claims '*One thing is needful.* – To "give style" to one's character – a great and rare art!' (232). This second declaration might initially appear to contradict the first statement, since it suggests that, rather than revealing a true self, we fashion our selves, make our selves up, 'style' our selves in whatever manner we wish. However, Nietzsche is asking that we 'give style' to our characters, and the sense is opened up of taking control of the self, understanding it, and styling it within these constraints. The alternative is taken up by 'weak characters' who are dissatisfied with their selves and consequently are resentful. This all ties in with another idea introduced in *The Gay Science* and which is further discussed in *Thus Spoke Zarathustra*: *amor fati*, 'love of fate'. By this is meant, at least within Nietzsche, a grasping of one's own destiny. The combination of all these elements would suggest that one's self-overcoming in a movement towards the true self is in itself an embracing of one's own fate and of thus being authentic.

It is within this idea of authenticity that Nietzsche's doctrine of Eternal Recurrence might be best understood, as a means of testing the authenticity of an individual's existence:

> What, if some day or night a demon were to steal after you into your loneliest loneliness and say to you: 'This life as you now live it and have lived it, you will have to live once more and innumerable times more; and there will be nothing new in it, but every pain and every joy and every thought and sigh and everything

unutterably small or great in your life will have to return to you, all in the same succession and sequence – even this spider and this moonlight between the trees, and even this moment and I myself. The eternal hourglass of existence is turned upside down again and again, and you with it, speck of dust!' (1974: 273)

How you respond to this with respect to the life you are leading is an indication of how 'authentic' it is. If to repeat current actions forever would fill you with horror, then there is clearly something wrong, whereas if you can desire this, then there is the 'yea-saying' to life that Nietzsche promotes so forcefully in *Thus Spoke Zarathustra*. In *Beyond Good and Evil* it is the 'life-affirming man' 'who wants to have it again *as it was and is* to all eternity, insatiably calling out *da capo* [again, from the beginning] not only to himself but to the whole piece and play' (2003: 82). Sartre has an interesting twist on this notion of forcing the individual to take stock of his or her life at every given moment and judging it against the measure of eternal recurrence. In his play *No Exit* the character Garcin complains that he has died too soon, in the sense that he has not lived long enough to realize his dreams of the person he wished to be. Inez, one of the other characters he is consigned to spend his time in hell with, replies: 'One always dies too soon – or too late. And yet one's whole life is complete at that moment, with a line drawn neatly under it, ready for the summing up. You are – your life, and nothing else' (Sartre, 1989: 43). In other words, we are not what we intend otherwise, we are what we are and what we have lived to be up to this very minute. Sartre's vision is an inversion of 'eternal recurrence': rather than asking 'Would you be happy to live these moments over and over?' Sartre asks 'Would you be happy to have your life judged from this endpoint?'

The Body and Self

Although the first part of *Either/Or* addresses the sensual nature of human beings, as does the 'In Vino Veritas' section of *Stages on Life's Way*, there is little else in Kierkegaard which suggests a preoccupation with the body, with the biological self or with physical health as a determinant of philosophy or psychology. The self's project in Kierkegaard often begins with explorations of psychological states which are intellectual in nature, and even in *Either/Or* Volume there is something distant in regarding such behaviour as belonging to the aesthetic sphere – a dandification of the self. For Nietzsche, however, philosophy is rooted in the body. In his Preface for the second edition of *The Gay Science* (1887; first edition 1882), he tells the reader that the spirit of the book is one of the convalescent glad to be back in health: 'This whole book is nothing but a bit of merry-making after long privation and powerlessness, the rejoicing of strength that is returning, of a reawakened faith in a tomorrow and the day after tomorrow' (1974: 32), and goes on to consider whether all those philosophies which strive for religious or aesthetic transcendence are not in essence driven by some sickness of the philosopher: 'and often I have asked myself whether, taking a large view, philosophy has not been merely an interpretation of the body and a *misunderstanding of the body*' (34–5). But does this have any place in Existentialism?

I began this book by saying that Existentialism starts with the self, even as it acknowledges 'self' as a part of a social world populated by others. But what exactly constitutes that self is open to question and has lacked any authoritative definitions. The dominant line in Existentialist thought is that the self is to do with phenomenological psychology, perception, mind and an inner authenticity which the self recognizes: it would appear to be, in more modern terminology, primarily about self as 'consciousness' and awareness of a future 'self' to be realized, revealed or unfolded over time. Nietzsche's emphasis on the body is in distinct contrast to the more usual Existential emphasis on consciousness. He regards consciousness as the most recent component of the human organism and thus its least developed, and claims that it is an illusion to take it 'for the "unity of the organism"' (85). What can be said with regards to Nietzsche is that there is a sense of organic unity for individuals, but that this is not derived from consciousness, but from an engagement with the world of a more visceral kind. The Kierkegaardian strand of Existentialism has an emphasis on the inner self, whereas the Nietzschean strand has a physical and mental yea-saying which seizes its self and seizes the world. It is the former which finds its way in a modified form into Heidegger and the latter into Camus, and it is a tension between the two which is manifest in Sartre, with an increasing bias towards engagement with the world in parts of *Being and Nothingness* and later works, once he has moved away from his earlier psychological view. But from Nietzsche as a whole, the idea that what is true is that which is subjectively valuable or significant, and that the individual is free to define this over and against the common lot, echoes Kierkegaard and paves the way for later Existential thinkers.

NOTES

1 *The Gay Science*. Kaufmann, the editor, notes: 'Nietzsche derived this motto from Pindar, Pyth. II, 73, and later gave his *Ecce Homo* the subtitle: "How one becomes what one is." Cf. also Hegel's formulation that "spirit . . . makes itself that which it is" ' (1974: 219).

CHAPTER 4

HEIDEGGER (1889–1976)

In the history of philosophy it is Heidegger who places 'Being' at the céntre of philosophical investigation. *Being and Time*, published in 1927, is his main philosophical work and the one that was most influential in the development of Existentialist thought, prompting as it did Sartre's own main Existential treatise, *Being and Nothingness*. Although Heidegger's later work continues to have Being at the centre of its enquiry, it is often characterized as making language the primary concern. He also sought to distance himself from Sartre and Existentialism and so it is *Being and Time* which remains the key text, introducing or foregrounding concepts which are central to Existentialist thought: 'authenticity', 'finitude', 'thrownness', Dasein, 'care'. We will look at the arguments Heidegger presents and develops in his rather formidable book.

Being

The book begins by saying that philosophy has taken for granted, misunderstood and diminished how 'existence' can be thought about, an error which has come down to us from the ancient Greeks. He argues that rather than ignoring existence or treating it in a lesser sense, we should be astonished by the very fact of existence. In the sentence 'The sky is blue', for example, it is the word 'is' that should command our attention, it is the 'isness' which is everything and which needs to be thought about (1995: 23). The problem is, or has been, that we do not notice the 'is' in the sentence at all, and yet the 'is' is the precondition for everything, for all 'entities', it is Being itself. So *Being and Time* sets itself the task of answering what it regards as the most fundamental of questions: 'What is the meaning of Being?' (19)

Unfortunately, if Being is the 'isness' of everything then it is in a way both everything and nothing – it is all-pervasive, since 'is' must be the condition of the universe. There is thus a vagueness to it which means that in seeking to answer the question, we are best advised to fix on something in which Being is manifest; we need some entity through which Being can be understood. Heidegger here suggests that there are different modes of Being and that for humans their particular mode of Being is 'Dasein', or to put it in more strictly Heideggerian terms, humans 'have the character of Dasein', and this distinctiveness is worth investigating (32).

'Dasein' literally translates as 'there-being' (usually written 'being-there'). It carries with it the sense that in Dasein, Being is present to itself *as Being* and is aware of itself as Being, it has a 'presentness' which is not the case with other types of entity. The reason for this is that Being is a question for Dasein itself; it asks itself, just as Heidegger is doing here, 'What is Being?', whereas Being is not a question for other entities. To put this into non-Heideggerian terms, humans are aware of themselves as 'existing' and ask themselves what it is to exist, whereas animals – a different type of entity from humans – do not. A dog does not ask itself 'What is it to be a dog?', or 'What is it to exist as a dog?' Therefore the kind of Being which distinguishes humans from all other kinds of Being is partly distinguished by the very asking of the question in the first place. So Dasein is a manner of Being which questions Being. No other entity does this, and in this way we can begin to understand Dasein in the sense of 'being-there'.

The attitude and behaviour – 'comportment' – Dasein adopts towards Being is what Heidegger calls 'existence'. The way Dasein understands itself is through this existence – but what precisely this existence is remains to be defined by each particular Dasein; it is not defined in advance:

Dasein always understands itself in terms of its existence – in terms of a possibility of itself: to be itself or not itself. Dasein has either chosen these possibilities itself, or got itself into them, or grown up in them already. Only the particular Dasein decides its existence, whether it does so by taking hold or by neglecting. The question of existence never gets straightened out except through existing itself. The understanding of oneself which leads *along this way* we call '*existentiell*'. (1995: 33)

It is therefore up to each Dasein to choose the possibilities of its own existence, the ways in which it will act with respect to the kind of Being Dasein represents. Another way of thinking of this is that although Being is general, the manner of 'being' for each person (strictly, each Dasein) is up to that individual, and this can only be worked out 'existentially', through existing, where 'existing' is understood under this idea of questioning Being.

But still, how are we to understand the Being of Dasein, how are we to understand its 'essential structures' (37–8)? Heidegger suggests we can understand it through observing its 'average *everydayness*'. This will allow us to begin to understand the Being of Dasein, although in a manner which is provisional, laying the ground for further analysis. Also, this analysis of Dasein will not in itself give us the meaning of Being. What gives Being meaning is 'temporality', the fact that Being is bounded, and bound by, time, and while we will need to reconsider all that is said about Being with respect to temporality, this will still only be a means towards understanding Being (38).

In calling the Being of Dasein 'existence', Heidegger makes clear that this mode of Being relates only to Dasein. The kind of existence that applies to 'a table, house or tree' is what Heidegger calls 'presence-at-hand', it is defined by the properties that constitute those entities and those properties are in essence fixed already (hence 'presence-at-hand'). This is not the case for Dasein. Each Dasein's Being has 'mineness' whereby there is nothing predetermined. Again, to put it in other (non-Heideggerian) words, each human individual's comportment towards their Being is 'owned' by them, is unique to them; each Dasein is a 'who' (existence) rather than a 'what' (presence-at-hand). Such existence therefore cannot be generalized, as it is with trees, houses and tables. 'I am' expresses precisely this sense of mineness in relation to Dasein's comportment towards its Being. And because Dasein is not something with predetermined properties, it is, rather, a comportment towards its Being in terms of its possibility:

> That entity which in its Being has this very Being as an issue, comports itself towards its Being as its ownmost possibility. In each case Dasein *is* its possibility, and it 'has' this possibility, but not just as a property, as something present-at-hand would. And because Dasein is in each case essentially its own possibility, it *can*, in its very Being, 'choose' itself and win itself . . . (1995: 68)

Being for Dasein is always 'Being-in-the-world', and this is part of the ontological structure of Being – 'the world' is not an optional extra, something tacked on to Being or something that Dasein can take note of or ignore at will. It is an ontological fact, an ontological given, what Heidegger calls an *existentiale*. And this Being-in-the-world is not in the same way as a table is 'in the world', it is not like a spatial property:

> From what we have been saying, it follows that Being-in is not a 'property' which Dasein sometimes has and sometimes does not have, and *without* which it could *be* just as well as it could with it. It is not the case that man 'is' and then has, by way of an extra, a relationship-of-Being towards the 'world' – a world with which he provides himself occasionally. Dasein is never 'proximally' an entity which is, so to speak, free from Being-in, but which sometimes has the inclination to take up a 'relationship' towards the world. Taking up relationships towards the world is possible only *because* Dasein, as Being-in-the-world, is as it is. (1995: 84)

Being-in-the-world also refers to the way Dasein disperses itself 'into definite ways of Being-in . . . having to do with something, producing something, attending to something and looking after it, making use of something, giving something up and letting it go, undertaking, accomplishing, evincing, interrogating, considering, discussing, determining' (83). What connects all these things, and their negative counterparts such as 'leaving undone, neglecting, renouncing' is 'concern' or 'care'. This is how the Being of Dasein is 'made visible', this is its Being-in-the-world. It is the way Dasein connects to the world, although again, this is not an option, it is an ontological given. It is important to stress that 'Being-in-the-world' and 'care' are part of the ontological structure of Dasein, since these must determine the way Dasein is. A non-Heideggerian formulation might perhaps regard this essential 'care' as something like the way in which, simply by being, we are engaged with (or in) the world.

Just as the type of Being that Dasein has is always Being-in-the-world and it is understood that there is no 'adding on' of the world *after* Dasein is considered, rather that 'Being-in-the-world' is integral to the ontological structure of Dasein, it is also the case that Being-in-the-world is always to be understood as Being-in-the-world-with-Others. Again, Heidegger is at pains to stress that the Others are not optional extras that we can choose either to acknowledge or to ignore, but Being is always a case of 'Being-there-too'. Nor does Heidegger mean this in the sense that Dasein exists alongside other objects in the world – the present-at-hand of Nature for instance – but it is part of Dasein itself: 'By "Others" we do not mean everyone else but me – those over against whom the "I" stands out. They are rather those from whom, for the most part, one does *not* distinguish oneself – those among whom one is too' (154) – 'the world is always the one that I share with Others' (155).

Now, the way in which Dasein is engaged with the world we have already seen is designated 'care' (*Sorge*). It is logical to suppose that the same relationship pertains between Dasein and Others, between Dasein and other Daseins. But care relates to a particular kind of entity, the present-at-hand (Nature) or the ready-at-hand (stuff, matter, equipment, gear), which has an ontical, factical existence rather than the ontological Being of Dasein. Thus the relationship between Dasein and Others is a particular kind of care which is usually translated as 'solicitude' (*Fürsorge*), meaning a concern for another's well-being. In our everydayness this is manifest in what we might regard as a negative way, since we often do not notice others, or they do not matter to us. For Heidegger this indifference is in itself part of solicitude. Again, solicitude is another *existentiale*, that is, a fact of Dasein's Being, part of the ontological structure of Dasein.

But this Being-with-Others also appears to be a Being-*for*-Others such that Dasein might lose itself in the Others, in the 'they', not because there is a Nietzschean herd mentality exactly, but because ontologically we are part of the 'they' and take pleasure in the same things, recoil from the same things, 'find "shocking" what *they* find shocking' (164). It is as if Dasein dissolves into the 'they', succumbing to the 'averageness' which the 'they' hold as their standard, and against which they are on guard for anything exceptional (164–5). But again, it should be stressed, this tendency to vanish into the 'they' is constitutive of Dasein, and in its turn 'reveals . . . an essential tendency of Dasein which we call the "levelling down" . . . of all possibilities of Being' (165) – it is not, therefore, something that can be eradicated; it is only something that can be guarded against. These pressures Heidegger groups together under the term 'publicness'.

A problem of the 'they' is that it lacks agency, so that while under the pressure of the 'they', there is no-one – no single person or group – who is responsible for this pressure. This also means that in dissolving into the 'they', Dasein is 'disburdened' of its Being: it is a comfortable thing to be accommodated by the 'they' for: 'Everyone is the other, and no-one is himself. The "*they*", which supplies the answer to the question of the "*who*" of everyday Dasein, is the "*nobody*" to whom every Dasein has already surrendered itself in Being-among-one-another' (165–6). Only when the Self is 'taken hold of' in its 'own' way will it be 'authentic', that is, not submerged in the 'they-self'. This is when it discovers its own authentic Being, its own 'who'.

It is at this point that Heidegger examines the 'there' of Being-there. Dasein is always 'there' in the sense of its 'Being-delivered-over to the "there"'. It isn't just 'there' in a static, neutral way; this 'Being-delivered-over' is what Heidegger calls 'thrownness', and this thrownness – again, an ontological given – is always present or uncovered or understood within a particular state-of-mind, a particular mood. Again, we are in the presence of an ontological given, since 'we are never free of moods' (175), and to overcome a mood is really only to replace it with another mood. Most likely this mood is in fact a turning away from the burden of Being.

There is another way in which Dasein fails to take hold of its Being. Being is always potentiality-for-Being, that is, 'possibility', yet Dasein will always already have let go possibility, or will have taken up its possibility-for-Being and made mistakes. Since Dasein is possibility-for-Being, it follows that Dasein is always involved in 'projection', it is always future-oriented in that Dasein is always understood (and 'understood' is part of Dasein's ontology) as possibility: 'projection, in throwing, throws before itself the possibility as possibility, and lets it *be* as such. As projecting, understanding is the kind of Being of Dasein in which it *is* its possibilities as possibilities' (185). There appears to be nothing specific meant here by 'possibility', in the sense of becoming something or someone particular, or fulfilling a particular role, as we might ordinarily understand the word. What is meant by Heidegger is more in the line that the nature of each Dasein is not fixed, Being is only a potentiality-for-Being, it is not a fixed entity. And if this is the case, it follows that we must already have let go of possibilities, while at the same time projecting possibility.

In returning to discuss the way in which Being-with-one-another means that the Self is absorbed into the world of the they,

Heidegger later in the book calls this 'fallenness'. He insists that this is not to be taken as a negative phenomenon, a 'not-Being'. Although it is a state of 'inauthenticity' it nonetheless represents a way of Being-in-the-world; in fact, 'fallenness' represents the kind of Being-in-the-world which is most usual (219–20). The world is tempting and can convince us that we are fulfilling ourselves. This has a 'tranquillising' effect, not necessarily in a soporific sense, but in a way that means we are pleased with the fullness of our lives in the belief that we have understood all. However, this understanding is only the understanding provided by the they, and, most likely unrecognized, this mode of Being is actually one of 'alienation', since the Self does not understand that it is fleeing from its Self. It thus has a sense of 'not being at home' – *unheimlich* – usually translated as 'the uncanny' but more literally, and in Heidegger's terminology, 'unhomely'.

How can Dasein understand itself under these circumstances? A further problem arises, then, in that Dasein comes to recognize that there can be no understanding of itself through the they, the recognition of which is manifest in 'anxiety'. The world is 'nothing' to Dasein, it is insignificant, and so Dasein, through anxiety, is thrown back on itself. It is this very nothingness of the world for Dasein's ownmost meaning, this sense that Dasein is '*Being towards* its ownmost potentiality-for-Being' (232) which creates anxiety. Again, as with other analytic terms in *Being and Time*, anxiety is constitutive of Dasein, it is an ontological given: '*That in the face of which one has anxiety . . . is Being-in-the-world as such*' (230). By throwing Dasein back on to itself, Dasein is individualized, it is 'for itself'.

Having got to a point in Division One of *Being and Time* whereby Being and Dasein have been analysed in structural terms, Division Two argues that this is as yet incomplete because we have not brought 'the *whole* of Dasein' into view, by which is meant that we have not understood Dasein in light of its having a 'beginning' – birth – and an 'end' – death. Is it possible to 'have' (grasp) the whole of Dasein? The immediate suggestion is 'no': because Dasein is a potentiality-for-Being, it must therefore '*not yet* be something' (276). To grasp Dasein in its totality would be to have in its grasp what is yet to be, it would be to 'fore-have'. But this is actually possible since the 'end' is always known, it is 'death', so that Being is always 'Being-towards-death' (277), and it is death that delimits Dasein. However, once again, we are not to understand 'death' in its everyday, 'ontical' sense.

We have a kind of objective view of death in the death of Others, since we know of or witness the death of Others. However, this cannot be a genuine understanding of death. Although it is an understanding of death as a biological event, and also perhaps as something more, since the rituals of mourning suggest we continue to exist 'alongside' that person, it does not have the significance that death does for each individual Dasein. It is perhaps here that what Heidegger means by 'mineness' is most evident, for clearly the 'end', and hence Dasein's whole, Dasein's totality, is only the end for each particular Dasein, and can only have meaning for each particular Dasein, understood in a unique way:

> Dying is something that every Dasein itself must take upon itself at the time. By its very essence, death is in every case mine, in so far as it 'is' at all. And indeed death signifies a peculiar possibility-of-Being in which the very Being of one's own Dasein is an issue. In dying, it is shown that mineness and existence are ontologically constitutive for death. Dying is not an event; it is a phenomenon to be understood existentially . . . (1995: 284)

By facing death, Dasein understands the possibility of its 'no-longer-being-able-to-be-there', it faces the impossibility of Dasein. But only by doing this can Dasein be *'fully* assigned to its ownmost potential-ity-for-Being' (294), at which point all relations with other Daseins are 'undone'. Again, the understanding of this rests on the sense of 'ownmost', the sense that in each Dasein's confrontation with its own Being-towards-death and with each Dasein's death there is something unique (and perhaps/probably incommunicable) about it which renders relations with other Daseins meaningless or irrelevant with respect to this. That does not mean that all of a sudden (or, indeed, structurally) Dasein as 'concernful Being-alongside and solicitous Being-with' no longer continues, for authentic Dasein can only occur when death is understood within these essential struc-tures of Dasein, for these structures shape the way in which Dasein comports itself towards its death. This taking on of its own death is also to be understood as a liberation for Dasein, since rather than being lost in 'the they', it is an acceptance of the finiteness of Dasein's ownmost possibilities (308). This recognition of Dasein's death – more specifically, the anticipation of it – is essential in revealing to Dasein how it is lost in the 'they-self' and so can then confront its being itself, without 'the they', and as such is a 'freedom towards death' (311).

But what is it that calls us to account, so to speak; what is it that makes us aware that we are lost in 'the they', that we are inauthentic? It is the 'call of conscience'. Again, with a term like 'conscience', which has a whole host of connotations in ordinary and philosophical language, Heidegger has to stress that he intends this term to have a particular meaning within his philosophy, so that conscience constitutes Dasein, it is part of its ontological structure. When conscience calls us to account, it shows us as Being-guilty. This conscience is not to be understood as a psychical phenomenon, such as 'understanding, will, or feeling' or a mixture of these (317). It calls the Self away from the 'they-self', and in so doing discloses to the Self its Being-in-the-world. Thus conscience is not what we would normally understand as a kind of inner Court of Justice, dependent upon a public and/or private morality; it is a matter of Dasein being called to account.

This leads on to a discussion of 'guilt'. While, as with all of these concepts, there is an 'everydayness' version whereby we feel ourselves guilty, perhaps in owing Others something or feeling responsible, these are 'ordinary significations' which belong to the realm of the inauthentic. Ontologically, primordially, guilt is something else which is constitutive of Dasein. Heidegger argues that guilt still carries with it the sense of 'lack', or, more precisely, a 'not', and he delves into this in some detail, uncovering these 'nots'. In the fact that Dasein is 'thrown' lies its (Existential) guilt, in a number of ways.

1. Dasein is 'thrown', and 'thrownness' is not an event that can be traced back in the manner of 'cause-and-effect', it does not have a historical origin – it is constitutive of Dasein. So, although Dasein is 'the basis of its potentiality-for-Being . . . it has *not* laid that basis *itself*'. In other words, Dasein does *not* ground itself, or through an act of will originate either itself or its thrownness; even though it 'takes over' its 'Being-a-basis', it is not its own origin. The guilt here lies in the fact that Dasein *never* has power 'over one's ownmost Being from the ground up'. Put most simply, 'Dasein is not itself the basis of its Being' – and once again

it is the 'not' which signifies the Existential guilt and 'nullity' (Existential nothingness, as opposed to the mere absence or lack of 'things') (330).

2. Dasein, as potentiality-for-Being, is always in one possibility or another. However, this must mean that it is *not* all the other possibilities. So while Dasein is 'Being-free', it can only have one possibility at the expense of *not* having the others.

3. There is a third possible sense of guilt in which the conscience that calls Dasein 'guilty' is also calling Dasein back from its lostness in the they. Although not specified in this section, the implication is that fallenness itself is 'guilt' (333).

It should be clear from this that 'guilt' is not something we happen upon every now and then, becoming guilty and then clearing our consciences, or failing to, as the case may be. Dasein is necessarily, structurally, guilty: '*Dasein as such is guilty*' (331) and is therefore a constant (353).

Guilt is an important concept in Existentialist thought and as an aside it might make more sense of Heidegger's account of guilt if we see how it is manifest more generally in relation to Existentialism. With respect to the first sense of Existential guilt discussed above, because we do not create our selves *as* being we are somehow 'nothing' – we cannot choose 'Being', Being is what is there. Secondly, even though we are free to choose our selves, or realize our selves in an authentic manner, or free to choose our lives, any choice must close off other possibilities, something about which we will feel guilty.

Having brought the philosophy to a stage where one is 'ready' to accept the Being-guilty, to accept the 'anxious' state of mind, Dasein is 'resolute'. Heidegger then builds on the notion of the authentic Being-one's-Self to provide what is essentially an ethics of co-existence, for this resoluteness:

> as *authentic Being-one's-Self*, does not detach Dasein from its world, nor does it isolate it so that it becomes a free-floating 'I'. And how should it, when resoluteness as authentic disclosedness, is *authentically* nothing else than *Being-in-the-world?* Resoluteness brings the Self right into its current concernful Being-alongside what is ready-to-hand, and pushes it into solicitous Being with Others. (1995: 344)

And by being authentic, Dasein's 'resoluteness towards itself' means that Others are able to ' "be" in their ownmost potentiality-for-Being': 'Only by authentically Being-their-Selves in resoluteness can people authentically be with one another' (344). (In passing we might note that this notion of all Daseins aiding each other in their authentic Being may seem at odds with the way Heidegger elsewhere characterizes Dasein's Being-in-the-world-with-Others as something essentially inauthentic. It is a point we will return to in Sartre and in Part Two of this book.)

All of this discussion is structured or bound by temporality, so that 'Resoluteness . . . is always the resoluteness of some factical Dasein at a particular time' (345). Here again Heidegger insists on the fact that Dasein is rooted in the world – it is not free-floating, isolated from the world. It is a mistake to believe that everything is possible. Dasein exists 'at a particular time' and so what is 'factically possible' is constrained by Dasein's temporality (or the temporality of Dasein) (345, 346). Heidegger designates this 'existential phenomenon' 'the Situation' – a concept we will see taken up by Sartre. The particular Situation that Dasein finds itself in is not one that it can choose; it is what is revealed by the call of conscience.

Heidegger identifies an impasse, however, in that the anticipatory nature of Dasein as Being-towards-death conflicts with resoluteness as a calling to potentiality-for-Being (349). The problem, although not quite spelled out like this, is that Being-towards-death suggests a fixity to one's ownmost Being which resoluteness contradicts in that the latter suggests an openness towards possibility rather than fixity. How can anticipation and resolution be brought together in anything other than a superficial manner? Heidegger seeks to solve this problem and to indicate the manner in which temporality is the basis of the unity of structure of Dasein.

Time

Temporality has three components: the future, the character of having been, and the Present. These are to be understood as different from ordinary conceptions of time which would divide into the future, the past, and the present, that is, a sequence of 'nows': a now which is currently happening, 'nows' which are yet to happen ('for the first time'), and 'nows' which are gone and so constitute the past.

The 'future' of existential temporality is given by the fact that Dasein's Being is '*Being towards* one's ownmost, distinctive potentiality-for-Being' and Being-towards-death (372). As such, Dasein comes towards itself – it is not 'future' in the sense that something is yet to happen and have a 'now'. Similarly, in taking over its thrownness, Dasein is taking over itself 'as-it-already-was', as it 'has been'. Again, an ordinary, inauthentic understanding of this notion of 'time' would suggest that this indicated Dasein's 'past'. But that is not the case. What is understood, more precisely, is that in taking over thrownness Dasein is always 'in the process of having been'. And third, what defines the authentic Present is the call away from falling, the being *there*, ' "the moment of *vision*" as regards the Situation which has been disclosed' (376).

There is one further reconsideration of Dasein's Being with regard to temporality, and that is its Being-towards-death. This should now be understood in terms of 'finiteness', or finitude. It is not that Dasein comes to an end, which would be to introduce an ordinary conception of time, but it is to say that Dasein's being is finite, and that everything is to be understood as finite. This is further emphasized when Heidegger talks about 'birth' as the other 'end' (425). Not only is Dasein Being-towards-death, but it is also Being-towards-the-beginning. Ordinarily, we might characterize Dasein as stretched between birth and death, filling up the allotted time span with a sequence of Experiences, of 'nows', and that such 'connectedness of life' is maintained by the Self's 'selfsameness'. But Existentially this cannot be the case for it would turn 'birth' and 'death' and 'now' into the present-at-hand, into 'objects' or 'entities'. For Dasein, 'birth' is not something which has happened in the past, something which was once a present-at-hand, just as 'death' for Dasein can never be an actuality. Instead, Dasein 'stretches itself along' between 'birth' and 'death'; Dasein is always already born, and, as we have seen, is already 'dying' in the sense of Being-towards-death. In this, Dasein is both 'stretched along' and 'stretches itself along': 'As care, Dasein *is* the "between" ' (427). Temporality, then, is not an 'entity' as such; it is the mode in which Dasein exists, fundamentally.

Heidegger's Language

There is no getting away from the fact that Heidegger is difficult. His language can appear quasi-mystical, and for those critics antagonistic towards him, it can verge on nonsense, with a strong suspicion that it probably is nonsense. Part of the difficulty is that in Heidegger meaning is offered provisionally, and built upon provisionally, so that even to attempt to paraphrase meaning becomes hazardous. The reason for this is that Heidegger advances a particular argument about the way discussion or philosophy should proceed, what is known as hermeneutics, 'interpretation', and for which Heidegger was largely responsible for bringing to the fore in the twentieth century. Briefly, when we consider a question we might put forward, the question will itself bring with it a host of assumptions – a 'horizon of understanding' – which in itself constrains the way we can talk about the question: 'Every enquiry is a seeking [Suchen]. Every seeking gets guided beforehand by what is sought' (1995: 24). This can lead to what may seem an incredibly convoluted thinking which does nothing else but avoid the question itself. A perfect example is the opening to his 1929 lecture, 'What is Metaphysics?':

'What is metaphysics?' The question awakens expectations of a discussion about metaphysics. This we will forgo. Instead we will take up a particular metaphysical question. In this way it seems we will let ourselves be transposed directly into metaphysics. Only in this way will we provide metaphysics the proper occasion to introduce itself. (2004: 93)

Here he second-guesses and forestalls his audience – he wants to surprise them into thinking about metaphysics in a way they might not have expected to do. But in ceding agency to metaphysics – as if it could 'introduce itself' – there is a suggestion, common in Heidegger, that rather than Heidegger himself demonstrating the point of the argument, the provisional truth of what is under discussion will bring itself forward of its own accord, will 'show' itself. This is similar to the way Heidegger conceives of Being, Dasein and ontological structure: these things are revealed in various ways, through anxiety, through moods in general, through our experience of averageness and everydayness. One reason for the difficulty of Heidegger's way of writing, then, is that to ask the question 'What is the meaning of Being?' as the fundamental question has within the question itself the answer, but how can this be revealed since we *are* this question?

Another reason for the difficulty of reading Heidegger is that language itself needs to be redefined, reconfigured, used in new ways. Heidegger's argument is that language has become habitualized, or our use of it is habitual, so that we no longer see or understand how it shapes the way we unconsciously perceive the world and existence. One of the ways in which Heidegger attempts to make us 'astonished' again at existence is thus by making the language we use seem unfamiliar or strange.

One strategy is to take a word and examine its etymology. The idea is that by tracing the history of a word back to its roots we achieve a purer ('primordial') understanding of the idea(s) carried within the word, perhaps meanings and concepts that have now been lost, distorted or taken for granted. It also, of course, serves to make the word unfamiliar so that we are forced to consider it in a new way. One example will suffice. In *Being and Time* Heidegger introduces the term 'phenomenology' and immediately splits this into its two components, 'phenomenon' and 'logos' (science) – thus the science of phenomena – and examines the meaning these words had in Classical Greek. It leads Heidegger to pronounce: 'Thus we must *keep in mind* that the expression "*phenomenon*" signifies *that which shows itself in itself*, the manifest' (1995: 51). Hence we come to understand 'phenomenon' itself in a new way. Both 'phenomenon' and 'logos' are then placed back into the original word, 'phenomenology', by which time we should have a very particular understanding of the word and what it stands for. Although the linguistic validity of such a method – the argument that a word's usage two thousand years ago can give us its meaning and usage now – is open to question, it undoubtedly achieves the effect of making the reader more attentive to the words in use.

If that were not enough, Heidegger believes that a new kind of 'grammar' is necessary to 'give a report' on Being (63). Although in translation the attempt is necessarily made to render the discussion readily intelligible, the difficulty of Heidegger's prose – in particular, I think, its circularity, whereby definitions often appear tautological, self-enclosed – is still evident. There is something, perhaps, of Kierkegaard's notion of 'indirect communication' in this aspect of Heidegger's language and in Heidegger's hermeneutical method. Both attempt to bring the reader to an understanding which cannot be reduced to the logic of the argument but is rather the reader's 'appropriation' of the writing.

To summarize . . .

I have focused exclusively on *Being and Time* here since its centrality to Existential thought is undoubted. It is a daunting book, easy to get lost in, but it is also a book in which Heidegger on occasion presents the reader with very useful recaps, and one towards the end of the book, Section 79 ('Dasein's Temporality, and our Concern with Time') is particularly helpful. I will use it to close this chapter while drawing parallels with Existential thought elsewhere.

The Section begins: 'Dasein exists as an entity for which, in its Being, that Being is itself an *issue*' (1995: 458). From Kierkegaard and Nietzsche we have seen that what is significant for philosophy is, or should be, 'actually existing individuals', our subjective make-up, however regarded. Heidegger's formulation is explicitly ontological, it is about Being and about the particular kind of Being which he designates Dasein. Dasein understands itself as projected forward on the basis of a 'potentiality-for-Being', and at the same time realizes that it is already 'there' in a manner not of its own making or willing. Here we can see Kierkegaard's movement forward on the basis of either/or, and Nietzsche's self-overcoming. In Heidegger's projection, in its potentiality-for-Being, Dasein discovers itself as 'thrown' and takes up this 'thrownness' through 'concern'. In its 'being with Others, it maintains itself in an average way of interpreting – a way which has been Articulated in discourse and expressed in language'. This is the world of the they, which in its everydayness reveals Being. Our concern finds itself 'grounded in temporality', and is conceived as a now, a presentness which concerns itself with 'awaiting' (things are about to happen) and as 'retaining' (former occasions). There is comparison to be made with Kierkegaard and Nietzsche in the notion of the abandonment which can be said to be bound up in 'thrownness'. For Kierkegaard the either/or of existence – the absoluteness of choice – is completely within the realm of the individual: there is nothing 'behind' it, nothing that could otherwise ground it, certainly *not* God. And for Nietzsche we are abandoned, in a godless world, to creating our own values, distinct for each individual. In the following chapter on Sartre, we will see how such central ideas as being, self, nothingness, freedom, anxiety, inauthenticity and the situation all come to have defining moments within Existentialism.

CHAPTER 5

SARTRE (1905–80)

What defines Existentialism, according to Sartre, is the idea that 'existence precedes essence'. To illustrate this he asks us to consider the production of a paper-knife. The artisan who makes it already knows its purpose before he makes it, and conceives of its manufacture in the light of this. In this way its 'essence' comes first – its maker already knows what it is for. When people think of God as the creator of man they are usually imagining a similar process, whereby God first conceives of man and the purpose of man, and then sets about to create him: 'Thus, the conception of man in the mind of God is comparable to that of the paper-knife in the mind of the artisan: God makes man according to a procedure and a conception, exactly as the artisan manufactures a paper-knife, following a definition and a formula' (Sartre, 1973: 27). Even if we replace God with the idea of 'human nature', the general argument is the same, for then man becomes defined by whatever it is believed constitutes this pre-given 'nature'. Sartre's basic Existential argument is that this is not so at all, that in fact 'existence' comes first, without definition, and finding that we exist, it is only subsequently that we go on to define ourselves. Further: 'If man as the existentialist sees him is not definable, it is because to begin with he is nothing. He will not be anything until later, and then he will be what he makes of himself' (28).

This is the somewhat simplified version of Existentialism that Sartre presented in the Paris lecture he gave in 1945 and which helped to popularize the new philosophy and make his own name synonymous with it. This central notion of man being essentially 'nothing' but what he makes of himself had been arrived at after a considerable body of work. His major opus to that point was *Being and Nothingness*, published two years earlier, and with a claim to being 'the bible of existentialism', but also steeped in Existential ideas had been his novel *Nausea* (1938). In addition, the book imme- diately preceding *Being and Nothingness*, *The Imaginary* (1940), had provided much of the psychological groundwork in its discussion of the way consciousness 'imagines', and understanding consciousness had also been central to work before that in *Sketch for a Theory of the Emotions* (1937) and *The Transcendence of the Ego* (1939). Reading *Existentialism and Humanism* without knowledge of the previous work gives the impression that man as a mode of existence free to define his own being is a purely metaphysical argument. Yet the argument initially rests on the way Sartre understands consciousness, since it is only through his formulation of how consciousness is constituted and functions that we find 'nothing- ness', and it is precisely this nothingness which guarantees man's (Existential) freedom. We also find that the self, such as it is, is created via this consciousness *ex nihilo* (out of nothing). From this description it should be clear that Sartre's work does not hold to a separation of psychology and philosophy. Once we have grasped Sartre's view of how self, nothingness and freedom are intrinsic to his conception of consciousness, we can move on to the perhaps more familiar Sartrean Existential terrain of 'in-itself' and 'for- itself', 'bad faith', 'anxiety' and 'freedom'.

Consciousness

We have seen how Kierkegaard and Heidegger reject received notions of the self or Ego, and that they posit the self as a relational term. Sartre moves towards this position early on in his writings in *The Transcendence of the Ego*. He begins the book by stating that for most philosophers and psychologists the Ego (the 'I' or the 'self') is a thing to be found in consciousness as a kind of material presence where we can locate 'desires and acts' and that this Ego acts as a uni- fying force (2004d: 1). He rejects this notion, and argues that the Ego is in fact an empirical object which only exists 'in the world'. By this he means that whatever we regard the Ego to be is a public event, just as understandable to a third person as it is to the person who has the Ego, and that this understanding is rather insignificant in compari- son to my consciousness (much of this exists as a direct refutation of Freud's view of consciousness). What is essential to my conscious- ness in effect remains untouched by any notion of an Ego, and at the same time, while I can know another's Ego since it is open to observation, I certainly cannot know another's consciousness: 'In a word, Peter's *me* is accessible to my intuition as it is to Peter's and in both cases it is the object of inadequate evidence. If this is so, there is nothing "impenetrable" left in Peter, apart from his consciousness itself. But this consciousness is *radically* impenetrable' (44–5). The rejection of the Ego (the 'I' and the 'me') would seem close to Nietzsche's rejection of the term when he considers it to be nothing more than a grammatical convenience, a way of referring to some-thing that is doing something. What we have instead of the psychologist's Ego is consciousness, which is impersonal and spon-taneously creating from one moment to the next. In Sartre's scheme, consciousness, up to and including *Being and Nothingness*, is king. It is through consciousness that we are aware of everything, and this continuous flow of consciousness (or rather 'consciousness*es*' created continuously) is beyond our control: it is spontaneous and overflowing. In fact, Sartre argues, when we realize that conscious-ness is like this, it engenders an anxiety in us, since we are faced with the knowledge that we do not create or will this consciousness, and hence we fabricate an Ego and (Freudian) unconscious with which we can 'mask' this truth and convince ourselves that we can conquer consciousness, that we, by way of an Ego, do control and create:

> I can thus formulate my thesis: transcendental consciousness is an impersonal spontaneity. It determines itself to exist at every instant, without us being able to conceive of anything *before it*. Thus every instant of our conscious lives reveals to us a creation *ex nihilo*. Not a new *arrangement* but a new existence. There is something that provokes anguish for each of us in thus grasping, as it occurs, this tireless creation of existence of which we are not the creators. On this level, man has the impression of eluding himself ceaselessly, overflowing himself, surprising himself by a richness that is always unexpected, and it is, once again, the unconscious to which he gives the task of accounting for the way in which the *me* is thus surpassed by consciousness. In fact, the *me* can do nothing to master this spontaneity, since *the will is an object that is constituted for and by this spontaneity*. (2004d: 46–7)

The portrayal of all that we might regard as valuable to our sense of self as an illusion that hides the truth of our non-selves is a recur-rent theme in Sartre. It is nuanced differently in *Being and*

Nothingness, as we shall see, since at some point Sartre must argue that we find ourselves engaged in the world in specific ways, and can do so in good faith. But the idea that there is no essential self can be seen here as a consequence of the way consciousness is produced and operates and the anxiety it produces.

Sartre further attacks received ideas about our psychological constitution in *Sketch for a Theory of the Emotions* but rather than continuing to attack a notion of the self completely, he incorporates the Heideggerian concept of 'mineness', although this can also be seen as a continuation of the idea that it is each individual consciousness which is radically different, unknowable and impenetrable. In this book he challenges the common psychological idea that emotions are a disturbance in the body which we then later register and label. Again, for Sartre, it is consciousness that holds the key, and he asserts that emotion is a type of consciousness, a way of directing ourselves towards the world: 'Emotion is a specific manner of apprehending the world' (2004c: 35). It is rather like Heidegger's 'moods' in this respect, an orientation of Dasein. Hence it has a cognitive function, it is how we come to know the world, or, more accurately, it is how we come to present the world to ourselves. He urges, following on from Husserl,[1] that we focus entirely on the contents and process of our consciousness: 'It is this consciousness that must be interrogated; and what gives value to its answers is that it is *mine*' (8). He talks of the investigator's 'proximity' to consciousness; this is the interrogation of the individual's consciousness by the individual, this is what is absolutely 'impenetrable' to others, and Sartre quotes Heidegger: 'The existent that we have to analyse . . . is ourselves. The being of this existent is *my own*' (8–9). Sartre continues to follow Heidegger's line and stresses the role of choice in Dasein's 'assumption' of this understanding of being. Emotion is, therefore, not something 'extra' to consciousness, it is not a 'psycho-physiological disorder' (13); it is a consciousness and as such can reveal being to human-reality (Dasein). Further, what the emotion means for the human-reality cannot be the result of influence by external forces. The significations discovered in emotion are embedded within the emotion itself as constituted by consciousness (30ff.).

In discussing the way emotion is consciousness directed towards the world, Sartre also states that the emotion-consciousness is a link between consciousness and world, since consciousness is always, as

Husserl states, consciousness *of* something. So if my emotion is hate, it is hatred *of* someone, directed at an object: 'The emotional consciousness is primarily consciousness *of* the world' (34), consciousness and the world are inextricably linked. This is an important point to note, since we can see that Sartre's understanding of consciousness is not as some entity which creates the world as a fiction of its imagination, but which is 'in' or 'alongside' or 'with' the world at all times. Sartre goes on to say that emotion-consciousness transforms the world when it encounters difficulties. We have a cognitive ('hodological') map of the world, which presents itself with pathways and obstacles, rather like a pinball machine, and when we become frustrated, for instance, by not being able to go in one particular direction, the emotion-consciousness transforms into a different emotion-consciousness (38ff.).

It was said above that consciousness is spontaneous. It should be noted, however, that it is not 'spontaneous' in the sense it can simply choose to do what it wants, 'free to deny a thing and to affirm it at one and the same moment' (52–3). This is because in transforming the world via emotion, there is an inherent 'belief' involved in this orientation; otherwise, to become involved in a gratuitous willing would amount to what Sartre will elsewhere call 'bad faith'. It cannot be spontaneous in this sense because consciousness and world are, as we have already said, inextricably linked: 'It *knows* itself only in the world' (53). To simply choose something other than this would be arbitrary, not spontaneous. Sartre is always explicit that consciousness takes place in the world – it is not detached or isolated. This relation between consciousness and world, and the nature of freedom that is embedded in the relation, is clearly marked in *The Imaginary*.

The initial distinction that this book makes is between 'perception' and 'imagination'. When I look at a chair in a room I perceive it, or, in Sartre's terms, the consciousness that I have is a perception-consciousness. If I now close my eyes and imagine – 'image' – the chair, my consciousness is an imaging consciousness; more precisely, it is not an image of the chair I produce but 'the-chair-as-imaged' (2004b: 6ff.). He argues that perception and imaging are radically different processes, that the image presented to me when I close my eyes is not simply a weaker version or imprint of the originally perceived chair. Even though the object, the physically present chair, is the same in perception and imaging, rather in the way that emotion is apprehended in emotion-consciousness in *Sketch for a Theory of the Emotions*, the 'image' in the activity of imaging is constituted and apprehended simultaneously.

Guiding *The Imaginary* are these questions: is the ability to imagine an extra faculty of consciousness, a 'contingent enrichment' which we could just as easily survive without (2004b: 179), or is the ability to image (to have in consciousness things which are not physically before us as they are in perception) 'an essential structure of consciousness' such that without it we would not be what we are, and consciousness itself would not be consciousness?

In working towards a conclusion, Sartre identifies the image (the mental object) as 'irreal', that is, it is not in the world, it is imaginary in consciousness, or, more strictly speaking, it wholly constitutes the imaging consciousness. It does not, therefore, depend upon the world, even if initially it is derived *from* the world. The significance of this becomes clear: this is the source of our freedom. If we did not have the ability to imagine, to produce the imaginary, we would be condemned to whatever was given to our perception, we would be condemned to what Sartre calls realism, to accepting the world as it is, since we would have no mechanism for doing or being otherwise. But we are also faced with something else if we recognize that the image is irreal and that we are responsible for producing it, for creating it. It means that it is based on nothing, that the object of the imaging consciousness has no material existence. When we perceive something as in front of us, as both real and present, there is an intrinsic belief involved that it is precisely of this nature. When we image (imagine), the corresponding intrinsic belief is that the image is precisely a nothing, that is, it is not believed to be anywhere in the real world, even if some aspect of it is a reference to a real-world object. So when I image, Sartre states: 'the imaging consciousness posits its object as a nothingness' (11). Thus the basis of our essential freedom, as revealed through the structure of the imaging-consciousness and the image, is nothingness. At the same time, the imaging consciousness has a non-reflective awareness of itself as producing these images spontaneously, hence, out of nothing. So the imaging consciousness is doubly caught up in nothingness:

> . . . an imaging consciousness gives itself to itself as an imaging consciousness, which is to say as a spontaneity that produces and conserves the object as imaged. It is a kind of indefinable

counterpart to the fact that the object gives itself as a nothingness. The consciousness appears to itself as creative, but without positing as object this creative character. (2004b: 14)

In fact, Sartre goes on to make a more radical suggestion, which is that the imaging consciousness does not have an 'image' in it, as if there were a collection of objects there among which we would find a particular image, but that the image itself *is* the consciousness; it is not subsumed within a larger consciousness.

But the role of nothingness does not end with (1) the imaging consciousness's awareness of itself as spontaneously creating out of nothing and (2) the 'object-as-imaged' posited as a nothingness. To image is also to set the object-as-imaged (the image) in opposition to the world, it is to know that the imaging consciousness presents to itself an image that is detached from the world and thus to make (apprehend) the world as nothing in relation to it. To image is both to nihilate perception and to nihilate the world: 'For consciousness to be able to imagine, it must be able to escape from the world by its very nature, it must be able to stand back from the world by its own efforts. In a word, it must be free' (184). Here Sartre indicates his complete agreement with Heidegger as to the interrelation between world, freedom and nothingness:

So to posit the world as world and to 'nihilate' it are one and the same thing. In this sense Heidegger can say that nothingness is the constitutive structure of the existent. In order to be able to imagine, it is enough that consciousness can surpass the real and constitute it as a world, since the nihilation of the real is always implied by its constitution as a world. (2004b: 184)

Again Sartre warns against any notion of arbitrariness in this freedom from, and nihilation of, the world. Freedom and nihilation only occur in relation to the world, only occur because we are in-the-midst-of-the-world; the imaging consciousness only occurs in relation to a specific world which we posit as a whole, as a synthetic unity, at the same time as we distance ourselves from it, at the same time as we surpass it. Freedom is therefore produced within specific circumstances, it is always in 'a situation', it is always 'in situation'.

For Sartre, then, man encounters himself through consciousness, or is constituted by (or in) consciousness, is 'free' in this respect, while this freedom is founded in various ways on a nothingness which is embedded in the existent, and which is always situated. Sartre's assumption is that 'being' is the 'thinking subject' in the form of consciousness, and this is at the centre of all his discussions to do with being and existence. This is distinct from Heidegger who, according to Sartre, puts 'the question of being' at the centre of being and thus fails to take enough account of consciousness (85). But what does this 'consciousness of being' amount to? It is in *Being and Nothingness* where Sartre takes his thinking fully into the realms of metaphysics, while never losing sight of his psychological groundwork, and where he provides an extensive treatment of human existence beyond the specific instances of Ego, emotion and imagination. It is here where Sartre argues that being, or consciousness – the two are often interchangeable in Sartre – consists of the 'for-itself' and the 'in-itself' and *Being and Nothingness* sets out to describe the relationship between these two categories in Sartre's overarching Existential schema. It is, in effect, Sartre's own version of the central Existential idea that the self (being) is a 'relation' which has no grounding and is not its own origin, rather than an 'entity' which has, or is, 'substance', as when man is considered as God's creation or as having an essential human nature. We will also see that Sartre develops his ideas about nothingness further, and that nothingness continues to be fundamental in ways additional to those above through the manner in which the self, or 'existent', is constituted.

The 'In-itself' and the 'For-itself'

The 'in-itself' (*en-soi*) is the thing I am, it is what I am before I begin to think about what I am, it is the 'pre-ontological' consciousness. The 'for-itself' (*pour-soi*) is that mode of consciousness which thinks about the 'in-itself', or, to put it another way, is that mode of consciousness which considers its 'self', which thinks about 'me'. My existence, therefore, is the relationship between the thing I am (the 'in-itself'; being) and the thinking about (consciousness of) the thing I am (the 'for-itself'; consciousness of being).

There is a problem here, since this seems to suggest that there are two different notions of what I am. Surely whatever I am *includes* the thinking about the whatever it is that I am? Which is precisely the issue: there is a gap between the entity thought about, the 'in-itself', and the entity which is conscious of itself as existing, or conscious of itself as a consciousness, the 'for-itself'. I thus find myself in the world, I 'encounter' myself, and yet even though I did not create this self or bring this self into existence, I nevertheless find that I am responsible for it.

To put the problem in more personal terms, I might ask myself 'Who am I? Who is Steven Earnshaw?' The answer should be self-evident, to me at least, since I *am* Steven Earnshaw. And yet the answer is not immediately forthcoming. The gap here is between that part of me (my consciousness) which is questioning the nature of existence of Steven Earnshaw (the for-itself; the consciousness of Steven Earnshaw), and the very entity which is being asked about (the in-itself; 'Steven Earnshaw'). Steven Earnshaw, therefore, both is and is not that Steven Earnshaw that is being thought about.

One vivid example Sartre gives to illustrate this is of a peeping-Tom who observes through a key-hole an infidelity being played out. He is completely absorbed in the scene. But then suddenly the voyeur hears footsteps and immediately becomes aware of himself. Before the approach of another person the voyeur is 'in-itself', he is not thinking 'I am a voyeur', he simply *is* a voyeur. Only after hearing the footsteps does he reflect on his being a voyeur, only then is it brought to consciousness and he might begin to feel guilt. As soon as that happens, the gap opens up between the 'in-itself' (the unself-conscious voyeur) and the 'for-itself' (1995: 260).

Sartre believes that being has a fundamental desire to close the gap, to make its reflecting on its being the same thing as the reflected-on, to make the two one-and-the-same, to make them 'coincident'; hence, consciousness of who or what I am would be the same as that 'who' or 'what' which my consciousness believes me to be; there would be no distance between the two. Yet the only creature that could possibly have such a self-coincidence is God (or a god), since a creature that self-created would have no gap between the in-itself and the for-itself; it would be its own origin, it would be, in Sartre's terms, a 'in-itself-for-itself'. Let us look at the 'for-itself' in more detail.

When I ask the question 'Who is Steven Earnshaw?' but do not immediately have an answer, this might simply be put down to the fact that I am a complicated person, or psychologically unstable, or unsure of what career I would like to follow. But Sartre's analysis of the nature of being is much more fundamental than this. Putting my self under question occurs because I am not predefined in any way; although I find that I exist, there is *nothing* to say what defines that existence, there is *nothing* to say who I am. This means that I am free, therefore, to define my existence, to make or determine my self. But this in itself is a source of 'anguish' since it conflicts with the desire to simply 'be', the desire of the 'for-itself' to coincide with the 'in-itself'. Sartre gives another couple of examples to illustrate these points about anguish, freedom, nothingness, and the groundlessness of self. The examples also serve to illustrate how what we consider the 'future' and the 'past' are also not fixed in any way.

In the first example, Sartre imagines himself walking alongside a precipice on a path that has no guardrail (30ff.). He looks into the abyss and experiences fear (of falling), and through this fear is made aware of his 'anguish' about his existence. Sartre is worried he might slip on a stone and is therefore aware that he may not be the origin of his own destruction. He can avoid this by paying careful attention to the ground and by moving as far away as possible from the edge. But it does not end there. There is a realization that simply knowing these possibilities, which are *my* possibilities, is not enough, for just as I may pay greater heed to the perceived danger, I also realize that this is not in itself sufficient to determine that I will act in this way. I might choose the course of action that tips me into the abyss. In considering these possibilities, I imagine a future self, which I am not yet.

I am not the future self in three ways. (1) I am separated from it by time. (2) 'I am not that self because what I am is not the foundation of what I will be.' (3) 'I am not that self because no actual existent can determine strictly what I am going to be.' He concludes:

> If *nothing* compels me to save my life, *nothing* prevents me from precipitating myself into the abyss. The decisive conduct will emanate from a self which I am not yet. Thus the self which I am depends on the self which I am not yet to the exact extent that the self which I am not yet does not depend on the self which I am. (1995: 32)

By describing how the for-itself becomes aware of its self as without any kind of grounding, Sartre is able to emphasize how 'nothingness' 'haunts' being, how the self is 'free', but that this 'freedom' is accompanied by 'anguish', since who I am is part-constituted by who I project I will be, which in itself is indeterminate and indeterminable. In this way, in a phrasing which Sartre is fond of repeating throughout *Being and Nothingness*, 'I am what I am not' and 'I am not what I am'.

In the second example which illustrates the interconnection between being, anguish, nothingness and freedom, Sartre imagines a reformed gambler approaching a roulette-wheel (32ff.). He has renounced gambling freely and in all earnestness, and as such considers himself to be a reformed gambler, but now he is faced with the possibility that he will gamble again. What will stop him from gambling? Is it the fact that he has resolved to be a reformed gambler? No, for there is *nothing* to stop him gambling again if he wishes, and as soon as he starts thinking about this, there is a 'gap' or 'rupture' between the identity he believes himself to have or to be – the reformed gambler – and the consciousness for which this is now an object of contemplation: 'The resolution is still *me* to the extent that I realize constantly my identity with myself across the temporal flux, but it is no longer *me* – due to the fact that it has become an object *for* my consciousness.' There is *nothing* to stop him taking up gambling again, and although he might consider the dire consequences of gambling for his finances and for his family, just as he may have done previously in the run-up to becoming a reformed gambler, he must now do so as if it is for the first time; he must 'rediscover' or 're-create' these fears: '. . . I perceive with anguish that *nothing* prevents me from gambling. The anguish *is me* since by the very fact of taking my position in existence as consciousness of being, I make myself *not to be* the past of good resolutions *which I am*'.

Bad Faith

Once Sartre has identified, in a similar vein to Kierkegaard and Heidegger, that man is not his own origin, and must suffer the anguish of freedom in the face of nothingness, he fleshes out what it means in more concrete terms by looking at how we might behave once we have understood our predicament. For instance, it is only natural to try to flee the anguish, to try to resolve it in some way, and this can often lead to *mauvaise foi*, 'bad faith'.

One way of thinking about the desire for the 'for-itself' to be identical with the 'in-itself' is that I desire to be my true self. 'Be yourself', I think, and endeavour to be this self. Sartre argues that this is impossible, and to believe that it is possible, or for me to say that I have achieved such a state, is an example of 'bad faith'. It is, to use Sartre's example, rather like promising to be sincere, since I either 'am

sincere', and hence unaware of it, or am playing the role of being
sincere. Pierre wants to be a waiter, and he strives to make all the right
moves and gestures. But however he does it, he will always be playing
at being a waiter (1995: 60). As soon as I project my self into the
future, and imagine that I am become my true self, I clearly am not
that 'true self' now, since it is yet to happen, and if there were, theo-
retically, a moment when I became my 'true self', the awareness of it,
the being conscious of it, would automatically invalidate it, since to
be able to hold my 'true self' up to my self would be to treat it as an
object which could be posited in other ways. Thus all attempts to col-
lapse the 'for-itself' into the 'in-itself' are 'doomed to failure'.

It might be argued, however, that I experience things which just are
me, if I am sad for instance. But according to Sartre, and consistent
with his argument in *Sketch for a Theory of the Emotions*, 'sadness'
is in effect 'consciousness of sadness'; if I suffer, it is because I am
conscious of my suffering. So even though it seems that emotions fall
outside the argument that I 'make myself', that somehow emotions
reveal a real me, for Sartre they are revealed through consciousness
of them, which means that awareness of emotion is simultaneously a
positing of an emotion which might be posited in other ways. To put
it in a more Sartrean manner, emotion just is consciousness of
emotion – if I am happy, that is the same as saying I am conscious of
being happy, there is not some entity 'happiness' which precedes my
consciousness of happiness. And in Sartre's analysis, this also means
that I am free to change the emotion. If I am alone and sad, and
another person comes into the room, I can put on a 'brave face'; in
other words, I can choose the emotion. Similarly, therefore, I make
my own suffering: 'I find only *myself*, myself who moans, myself who
wails, myself who in order to realize this suffering which I am must
play without respite the drama of suffering' (1995: 92). The argument
is that because we have knowledge of our suffering – that is, have
some distance from it, or in a sense posit it – we are never totally overwhelmed by it, therefore it never achieves an in-itself, but is always a
for-itself, and hence Sartre can claim that we do indeed make our own
suffering (92).

Others and the Other
So far I have discussed being and consciousness as somewhat isol-
ated terms within Sartre's ontology. From Kierkegaard through to
Heidegger we have seen that there is always recognition of 'others',

the 'they', the 'public', the 'herd'. Sartre picks up on Heidegger's idea that 'being' is always 'being-in-the-world-with-Others', but notes that this is offered in the sense of an 'alongside others', so that although we are in the world with others, we are in a way remote from them. What Sartre offers instead is something more radical: in addition to the 'in-itself' and the 'for-itself', there is a crucial third term which suggests the absolute incorporation of the Other into structures of self: 'There is a relation of the for-itself with the in-itself *in the presence of the Other*' (1995: 361). If we return to the above example of the voyeur, we can see what he means.

The main argument here, one that is not present in the previous work discussed, is that we are only aware of being, or have consciousness, through, or because of, others. Until I am aware that I am perceived by an other, I do not have consciousness, therefore my consciousness is utterly dependent upon the presence of the other. Think of it from the opposite point of view. If I am alone (unobserved) I am not self-aware, such things as 'shame' and 'guilt' – as provoked by being discovered as a voyeur – cannot occur, or, as Sartre comically puts it: 'Nobody can be vulgar all alone!' 'Shame', 'guilt' (and 'vulgarity') are judgements brought to bear on myself, by myself, through the mediation of the Other: 'the Other is the indispensable mediator between myself and me. I am ashamed of myself *as I appear* to the Other' (222). Not only that, but the fact that 'shame' and 'guilt' are brought into being/consciousness by others indicates that my consciousness is affected by others, of necessity. Without the Other, 'there is no self to inhabit my consciousness, nothing therefore to which I can refer my acts in order to qualify them' (259). Without the Other, I would not have consciousness, and the presence of the Other affects what that consciousness is. In this way, awareness of the existence of the Other is pre-ontological (251).

In talking about 'the Other', Sartre introduces the notion of 'the Look'. To see the Other is in fact to 'be seen', to be aware of the self, and 'This means that all of a sudden I am conscious of myself as escaping myself, not in that I am the foundation of my own nothingness but in that I have my foundation outside myself. I am for myself only as I am a pure reference to the Other' (260). There are a number of consequences to this. I become aware of the freedom of the Other to fix me in a way which is beyond me, or which escapes me. I therefore present a face to the world which I cannot know, which I have no control over, and as such am not master of the situation that I find myself in. So I exist in the midst of the world, I 'live my self', in a way which I cannot know. Sartre here distinguishes his own view of being-in-the-world and others from that of Heidegger's, for while being-in-the-world is always 'being-in-the-world-with-others' for Heidegger, in the sense that it is part of the ontological structure of Being, Sartre does not consider the 'being-for-others' an 'ontological structure of the for-itself' (282). Essentially, the Other is an object for me and I am an object for the Other.

However, while being-for-others is not an ontological structure of Being, nevertheless, at the same time as I experience my 'upsurge' of Being, at the same time as I encounter myself, I am in relation with others. And since I am always an object for others because I am always 'being seen' by others (always under 'the Look'), my relation to others is through my awareness of my self as this object for others. Not only is there a sense of my contingency in that I am not my own foundation, but my self is also contingent in that it is made evident through the Other, and over this I have no control. The Other makes my self, and thus holds the secret of my self. Thus, even though I find myself as a 'being-for-others', I am not the foundation of this 'being-for-others'; the relation only exists because of the Other. It is on this basis that Sartre details our relations with others in the instances of 'love', 'masochism', 'desire' and 'indifference'. So, for instance, when I 'love' another, what I want to do, according to Sartre, is to appropriate the other's freedom, *as* freedom, so that while the object of my affections is free, my 'love' demands that within that freedom and of necessity, they should *freely* choose me as the beloved (366ff.). In that way would I be my own foundation, I would be coincident with the other's choice of me as my self. Masochism is the opposite of this – I attempt to become 'nothing' for the Other, that is, I aim not to be an object for the other so that I am not enslaved by the Other. In Sartre's eyes, this attempt must fail, for to want to be nothing for the Other is always dependent upon the Other. Which brings us back to the self. Just what, exactly, is it that my being is engaged in? What is it that should be so important to me? What is it that is 'me' and 'mine'?

The Project

'Freedom' and 'nothingness' are identical in Sartre's Existential scheme. I *am* nothing, because my existence precedes any essence, and I am nothing because what I am to be is yet to be decided, and so I am free to choose my self. Thus freedom and nothingness are interchangeable. This would seem to suggest that there is no basis for any particular actions I choose to become involved in, and, in fact, no basis for making any particular choices at all: I can choose to be who I want and what I want. Yet we have also seen that there is a necessity to be 'authentic', as if there is something which really is me which I need to be true to, something which is 'mine', or, to use Heidegger's term, something which is 'ownmost'. How am I to know what this is? And surely if it is 'mine' already, then in some sense I must already be fixed, otherwise there is nothing to be 'true' to. Furthermore, is it really the case that I am as free as Sartre suggests? After all, I find that I am a certain gender, class, race, age, *etc.*; I find myself 'in situation' in the way that Sartre insists on in both *The Imaginary* and *Being and Nothingness*; I appear to be constituted by facts over which I have no control and yet which substantially affect my existence. So, how am I to be 'authentic' yet free, and how can I be truly free in the first place when there are so many constraints on any freedom?

Sartre conceives of all these elements as operating as an 'ensemble' within the self's 'project'. For instance, 'to be', in Sartre's view, is 'to act', it is to perceive a lack in the world and to want to effect a change. This might suggest that we then look for the motive behind the intention-to-act in order to understand our selves. But for Sartre the envisaged change and the motivation for it occur simultaneously as an 'upsurge', a phrase which corresponds with our very 'upsurge' into the world. Both the act and the motivation, interdependent as they are, only have meaning through an overarching 'project', which, roughly speaking, is the way I orientate myself towards the future, the ends that I posit for myself. In this way, everything has meaning only through my 'project', a word and concept with immediate roots in Heidegger, and carrying with it both senses of a 'hurling forward' and an 'undertaking': 'It is therefore the positing of my ultimate ends which characterizes my being and which is identical with the sudden thrust of the freedom which is mine' (1995: 443).

This in itself would not answer the objections that I am neither wholly free nor sure of how I can be 'authentic'. There is a kind of recasting of the 'in-itself' and the 'for-itself' at this point. The 'in-itself' is the given of the self, it is part of my 'facticity', the brute fact of my existence. Similarly, I find myself in a 'situation', again, part of my facticity – for example, I am typing this book onto a computer in a room in a house in Sheffield in England. These are 'givens'. Yet as soon as I am conscious of these givens, of my facticity, I realize that I am free to alter them, that the given of the 'in-itself' is only revealed by my attempts either to flee it or be identical with it by way of my 'for-itself', that my being in Sheffield and writing this book is a given which I can change. And it is I who bring meaning to these givens, and am free to do so. There is always a pressure on me to say that the 'ends' I project for myself and which give meaning for me come from 'outside', 'from God, from nature, from "my" nature, from society' (440), but these are just pressures to hide my freedom from myself.

This notion of freedom might indicate that freedom is to be understood as 'arbitrary or capricious', since I can choose to stand up or sit down at will, do this or the other at will. Here, perhaps, is a common misunderstanding of Existentialism, that we are free to do whatever we like in a manner which is indeterminable and without basis. Sartre counters this by saying that the 'project' and the 'meaning' exist simultaneously, as if we are always 'in' the project and hence the meaning is always simultaneous with the project; it is not something that can be created at will out of thin air, irrespective of the project itself:

> This does not mean that I am free to get up or to sit down, to enter or to go out, to flee or to face danger – if one means by freedom here a pure capricious, unlawful, gratuitous, and incomprehensible contingency. To be sure, each one of my acts, even the most trivial, is entirely free in the sense which we have just defined; but this does not mean that my act can be anything *whatsoever* or even that it is *unforeseeable*. (1995: 453)

Sartre appears to have it both ways, to say that we are absolutely free, that being and freedom are interchangeable terms, and yet also to say that each act is never absolutely free, since it can only occur with respect to 'brute existents', to the facticity of my situation. But for Sartre it is impossible to separate out something that is pure 'facticity' from what may be freely willed: 'These observations should show us that the *situation*, the common product of the contingency of the in-itself and of freedom, is an ambiguous phenomenon in which it is impossible for the for-itself to distinguish the contribution of freedom from that of the brute existent' (488).

Sartre gives the example of looking at a mountain and deciding whether it can be climbed or not, whether it is 'scalable'. The question of its 'scalability' only arises because there is the project of climbing it; thus, although the mountain is undoubtedly there as a 'brute existent', how I conceive it is contingent precisely on my project with respect to it, and in this way both contingency (freedom) and facticity are locked together so that it is not possible to tell where one ends and the other begins (488). Likewise, Sartre explains, if I find my self resistant to some goal that I have, this certainly does reveal something of my 'given', of my 'in-itself', but only to the extent that it has meaning within the scope of this project or goal; it cannot mean that I have uncovered the true nature of my 'in-itself', since this meaning only occurs as a result of the project, just as the mountain does not intrinsically 'mean' anything, even as I recognize its facticity.

However, this still leaves us with the problem of determining what the project might be – how do I know what my project is, or how can I determine it? *Being and Nothingness* does not answer this directly. Instead, it works towards what it calls 'existential psychoanalysis', where, by applying the methods of psychoanalysis within the context of beings which are future-oriented – Sartre claims that psychoanalysis has no concept of the future – we can bring out, or at least sketch, the outline of our projects. It is by turning to *Nausea* that we can see just how such a project might be illuminated or arrived at, for it is in this novel where Sartre 'lives out' his ideas about Existentialism.

Nausea

Roquentin, the central character in *Nausea*, lives a relatively unencumbered life in Paris, drifting through cafés and casual affairs, researching a historical figure called Rollebon in order to write his biography. The novel begins with Roquentin's journal, and the first entries show us Roquentin attempting to get a grip on existence by describing exactly what he sees: 'The best thing would be to write down everything that happens from day to day. To keep a diary in order to understand' (Sartre, 1979: 9). It proves impossible; the phenomenological method – the bracketing out of the world in order to focus clearly and precisely on our apprehension of the world, without prejudice – cannot produce the experience and representation of *quidditas*, the 'thisness' of the world: 'For example, there is a cardboard box which contains my bottle of ink. . . . Well, it's a par-allelepiped rectangle standing out against – that's silly, there's nothing I can say about it. That's what I must avoid: I mustn't put strangeness where there's nothing' (9). It is not until some way into the novel that the nature of the world and existence is revealed to Roquentin in a municipal park: 'And suddenly, all at once, the veil is torn away, I have understood, I have *seen*' (181).

He is contemplating some chestnut trees in an unselfconscious manner and becomes overwhelmed by them to the extent that he no longer conceives of such things as 'roots' in terms of language, and everything, he realizes, just *is*; existence permeates everything. He also realizes that everything is 'superfluous', that there is no reason for its existence, including his own. Even to commit suicide, to remove the world of at least one superfluity, would simply leave the superfluity of 'decomposed flesh' (184–5), and further on he tells us that the Nausea he experiences is this realization that existence is 'contingency': 'I mean that, by definition, existence is not necessity. To exist is simply *to be there*; what exists appears, lets itself be *encountered*, but you can never *deduce* it' (188).

Towards the end of the novel, having come to the conclusion that writing Rollebon's biography has been a crutch to avoid existence, that clinging to his previous love, Anny, has likewise been a crutch, Roquentin finds himself: 'Alone and free. But this freedom is rather like death' (223). But at the end of the novel, the final revelation comes to Roquentin, what might be called his 'project'. It is to write the book that we have been reading, it is to write *Nausea*. The novel re-enacts the movement *Being and Nothingness* gestures towards in its discussion of 'project', that the project's meaning, or direction, or future, will emerge through the trials of life. And this also takes us back to the very beginning of *Being and Nothingness*, for it opens with a description of what an object is.

For Sartre, an object of perception is the sum of all its moments, such that it can never be known in its entirety. The coffee cup at the side of my computer is not fully revealed to me at any given moment since it also exists at other times and in other modes, so that I can only ever 'know' it partially at best. Similarly, our lives cannot be known until they are ended, and then they cannot be really 'known' since they are no longer 'existed' or 'lived'. However, there does appear to be a sense in Sartre that the life's 'project' emerges at death, rather than being fully revealed in the midst of life. Thus life, existence, must be a case of existing without full knowledge of one's project. In his novel *The Age of Reason* (1945), Sartre's first novel in the *Roads to Freedom* trilogy, the central character Mathieu characterizes being alive as 'consciousness', whereas our 'life' is the judgement made of us, or the story told of us, when we are dead (Sartre, 2001: 207). Coming at it from a different angle but with a similar conclusion, man 'is nothing else but the sum of his actions, nothing else but what his life is' (Sartre, 1973: 41), hence 'man is no other than a series of undertakings . . . he is the sum, the organisation, the set of relations that constitute these undertakings' (42).

Existential Praxis

The tension between thinking and doing is one which I highlighted in the Introduction, with Existential thinkers usually falling into one or other of the categories. In his most thoroughgoing Existential works, Sartre appears to hold the tension within himself. In his first play, *The Flies* (1943), the urgency is to rid ourselves of a crippling guilt, a guilt which we take on ourselves and are then happy to pass over to our rulers in order that we may be relinquished of responsibility for our actions. Thus we can evade any responsibility for our freedom. For Sartre, freedom is our *raison d'être*, and everything else is bad faith. Since that freedom is guaranteed by the nothingness which haunts consciousness and is the 'ground' of consciousness, it would suggest that our activity is primarily one related to the main processes of consciousness as categorized by Sartre – perception, imagination and thought. However, as early as *The Age of Reason*, freedom as a purely intellectual activity is shown to be somewhat empty. Mathieu is a philosophy teacher who maintains his freedom simply by not committing, either to his pregnant girlfriend Marcelle, or to the Communist Party. By not 'engaging', Mathieu is condemned to a fruitless 'waiting'. It is a portrayal of an Existentialist, or would-be Existentialist, who has held himself in readiness 'For an act. A free, considered act; that should pledge his whole life, and stand at the beginning of a new existence' (Sartre, 2001: 51). In his play *Dirty Hands* (1948), the central figure again is an intellectual. In this work the character does 'commit' by agreeing to murder somebody regarded as an enemy of the Party, only to find that he lacks the ability to get his hands dirty, to 'act'. We will see in Chapter 11 how Sartre re-envisages Existentialism (or abandons it, depending upon your perspective) in light of the necessity to act, in the necessity for 'praxis'. If it seems that we have been in the thick of Existentialism, thanks to Sartre, only to be left dangling, if 'free', with regards to how this might be taken further, that is because *Being and Nothingness* itself ends with a series of questions which Sartre claims fall under the domain of ethics, and any answers to which we must wait to find in another volume – a volume which never materialized. Before we pick that up again in Part Two, let us turn to Albert Camus, Sartre's one-time close friend and fellow traveller.

NOTES

1 See Chapter 9.

CHAPTER 6

CAMUS (1913–60)

The novel *The Outsider* and the treatise *The Myth of Sisyphus* are Camus's main contributions to the literature of Existentialism, both of which were written towards the end of the 1930s and the beginning of 1940, and both published in 1942. I will also discuss *The Rebel* (1951), since this builds directly on *The Myth* and develops a more socially oriented theory of the absurd, a movement paralleled in Sartre's move towards 'the social' as he subordinates Existentialism to Marxism in *Search for a Method* (1957) and *Critique of Dialectical Reason* (1960). Camus's inclusion within the canon of Existentialism has been questioned on occasion because his main focus is on 'the absurd', and, as we will see, it could be argued that the absurd as Camus defines it does not intrinsically entail an Existential viewpoint. Nor does Camus have too much to say about consciousness as such, and so does not fall within the phenomenological strand of Existentialism, although he is aware of this work in the Husserl–Heidegger–Sartre axis and occasionally presents his ideas in relation to it. Nevertheless, other critics automatically include him in the canon of Existential literature, and much of what Camus writes does fall within the domain of Existential thought. Investigating it here will also, therefore, allow us to explore Existential ideas from a different angle from previous chapters, and will thus also enable us to better mark the boundaries of Existential thought before moving on to Part Two, where we will trace the major themes of Existential thought.

'The Myth of Sisyphus'
Camus's essay is very open about its philosophic and writerly debts. There is mention and discussion of Kierkegaard, Nietzsche, Kafka,

Dostoevsky, Jaspers, Husserl, Heidegger, and Sartre himself, with whom Camus was a close friend until their public falling-out in 1952. The essay helps to identify in these writers, and other writers who have now fallen away, such as the 'Jewish-existential' philosopher Chestov, a 'family of minds' which, although using different methods, is unified by its assertion that the universe is not to be understood by science and reason. Camus brings to this his own approach, elaborating on his category 'the absurd', which starts with 'the problem of suicide'.

Suicide

Existentialism has sometimes had a reputation for being a rather depressing philosophy. This is not surprising given its reliance on such terms as 'anguish', 'alienation', 'despair', and 'finitude'. And even as Sartre later attempted in *Existentialism and Humanism* to refute the accusations that Existentialism was pessimistic, arguing that the opportunity to define ourselves and our future was just the opposite of despair, and de Beauvoir attempted to defend Sartre against the accusation in *The Ethics of Ambiguity*, Camus's *The Myth of Sisyphus*, at first glance, only reinforces the impression that Existentialism is prone to the miserable: 'There is but one truly serious philosophical problem and that is suicide. Judging whether life is or is not worth living amounts to answering the fundamental question of philosophy' (Camus, 2000a: 11). As Camus wryly notes, the answer for most people is 'yes', life *is* worth living, since they continue to live, although just what this 'living' consists of is what Camus questions. Paradoxically, he argues, it is those who commit suicide who are certain about life and its meaning, since they make their choice convinced that life is no longer worth the struggle, whereas the rest of us, mostly through habit, live on, unsure or unthinking.

From the outset, then, it is clear that Camus does not enter into philosophic discussion by way of consciousness or being – the staple terms we have used thus far in our outline of Existential thinking. Camus begins with his own category, 'the absurd', a recognition that the universe is without intrinsic meaning and hence all human endeavour is ultimately, viewed from this perspective, pointless. Faced with this, what values can we have that can make life worth living? The symbol Camus chooses is the ancient Greek mythical story of Sisyphus (107–9). Sisyphus is judged by the gods to have acted against them – there are different versions as to what incites this judgement – and his punishment is to roll a rock up a hill. Just as he is about to reach the top, the rock tumbles to the bottom. He is to traipse back down and begin rolling the rock up the hill again, and again and again, for all eternity. For Camus this is the situation humans find themselves in, this is their mutual condition, destined to labour on meaningless tasks without hope and for no reward. Why bother?

The Absurd

Camus describes the moment when we might arrive at this question, when we might be awakened to the true nature of our plight:

> It happens that the stage-sets collapse. Rising, tram, four hours in the office or factory, meal, tram, four hours of work, meal, sleep and Monday, Tuesday, Wednesday, Thursday, Friday and Saturday, according to the same rhythm – this path is easily followed most of the time. But one day the 'why' arises and everything begins in that weariness tinged with amazement. (2000a: 19)

This is, Camus notes in passing, Heidegger's 'mere anxiety'. He goes on to describe the kind of things that the awakened consciousness will notice. A man who has always put off things for the next day might suddenly realize that he is 30 and have intimations of mortality. He will be overcome with 'horror', 'tomorrow' will now become his enemy. At another level of awakening, similar to Roquentin's experience of the chestnut trees in the park in Sartre's *Nausea*, we might find the things of the world 'strange' and 'dense', 'sensing to what degree a stone is foreign and irreducible to us, with what intensity nature or a landscape can negate us' (Camus, 2000a: 20). Here is that sense of superfluity, the sense that there is no necessity for our existence, no necessity for our being. Similarly, others become strange to us, as if engaged in a world which we can no longer understand, part of a 'dumb-show', and consequently our image of what is human fails and we experience Sartre's nausea. And then, of course, we might encounter ourselves in the mirror or in a photograph, and be similarly estranged or alienated (21). He elaborates on this sense of self-alienation in a manner which foreshadows Sartre's *Being and Nothingness* and neatly captures the Existential view of self as relational:

For if I try to seize this self of which I feel sure, if I try to define and to summarize it, it is nothing but water slipping through my fingers. I can sketch one by one all the aspects it is able to assume, all those likewise that have been attributed to it, this upbringing, this origin, this ardour or these silences, this nobility or this vileness. But aspects cannot be added up. This very heart which is mine will for ever remain indefinable to me. Between the certainty I have of my existence and the content I try to give to that assurance, the gap will never be filled. For ever I shall be a stranger to myself. (Camus, 2000a: 24)

The absurd is a relational term. If in Sartre it is man who brings nothingness into the world, in Camus it is man who brings the absurd into the world. Camus gives an example of a man with a sword attacking a group of machine-guns, and it is the comparison of the two terms which produces the idea that the scene is absurd because there is a disproportion between the strength of the man and the strength of the group. Likewise, man encounters the absurd, or brings it into the world, when he attempts to understand the world (33). The absurd is thus the relational term between the confrontation of man and world, and both terms must be maintained in order to attempt an understanding of the absurd. Further, the absurd is the first truth for Camus, and any subsequent discussion on the subject must adhere to this truth. Because of this 'rule of method' – the necessity to abide by this fundamental truth – Camus is then in the situation of having to preserve the very thing that crushes him, having to engage in 'a confrontation and an unceasing struggle' (34).

Camus notes that some philosophers who have given a critique of rationalism and accepted the absurd, such as Kierkegaard, Chestov and Jaspers, have nevertheless 'forced hope' into the equation by way of the religious. Camus is very clear on this and reiterates throughout *The Myth of Sisyphus* that, in confronting and struggling with the absurd, man is to do so without hope. He is also clear that 'without hope' should not be taken to mean 'despair'. He asserts that it should be done without hope, like Sisyphus, because this means to stay with the truth of the absurd, the truth that there is no God or science which can save us, which could provide meaning and thus do away with the absurd. This is why Camus is so insistent upon his method – to let go would be to open up these 'escapes' from the absurd – and he subsequently insists upon (absurd) 'reason'. For Camus, these philosophers make the 'leap' to the religious at the very point where reason fails: Jaspers sees that the world is not revealed to man and so takes this to be evidence of the transcendent; Chestov argues that reason is useless so there must be something beyond reason; and Kierkegaard ultimately transforms the despair of 'antinomy and paradox' into the 'criteria of the religious' by letting go of 'the intellect' (35–40).

Camus finds a similar 'will to arrive' at a means of doing away with the absurd in the phenomenology of Husserl. The privileging of all moments and objects, removing from them the habitualized knowledge that prevents them being 'seen', is in accordance with the 'absurd spirit'. It restores depth and richness to the world. The leap of Husserl is then not religious but abstract, when in each perception he finds an eternal essence, with echoes of Plato (44–8). Both the 'abstract god of Husserl' and the 'dazzling god of Kierkegaard' are unjustified leaps towards a reconciliation between self and world, and both, as such, contradict Camus's rule of method, of persevering with only what we know. And more than that, the absurd man, in refusing all leaps beyond what is known, then 'wants to find out if it is possible to live *without appeal*' (53). With respect to Sisyphus, this is an essential component – that he should continue to roll the stone up the hill without appeal, with no expectation of any kind of external, eternal redemption.

In refusing the consolation of any kind of leap, including that of suicide since this too would serve only to repudiate the truth of the absurd, Camus asks for a permanent personal revolt. By this he means that we must live the absurd, and to live fully is to accept the absurd, it is to accept that there is no meaning. To 'live' is to always have the absurd in front of us, to contemplate it, to always have present our confrontation between the world and our 'obscurity': 'That revolt is the certainty of a crushing fate, without the resignation that ought to accompany it' (54). So far, so Existential. It is when Camus discusses the role of death in more detail, and his notion of freedom – so essential to Sartre – that there is some divergence from our discussion of Existentialism. Crucially, perhaps, as we will see, he does not offer a view of the individual as 'projecting' forward, for he argues that in the face of death there can be no 'future'.

Freedom

Camus regards all notions of freedom as illusory, for what or who would be the master from which we had freed ourselves? With respect to God, the case falls down when he considers the question of evil. If God is all-powerful and our master, then he must be responsible for evil, which cannot be true. If, on the other hand, we are free and bring evil into the world, then God cannot be all-powerful and hence cannot be our master (2000a 55). On a more mundane level, the man who considers himself free in the sense that he can direct his life, that his life has a sense of purpose, once awakened to the absurd and to the fact that he could die at any moment, becomes aware that this 'freedom' is a lie:

> Thinking of the future, establishing aims for oneself, having preferences – all this presupposes a belief in freedom, even if one occasionally ascertains that one doesn't feel it. But at that moment I am well aware that that higher liberty, that freedom *to be*, which alone can serve as basis for a truth, does not exist. Death is there as the only reality. (2000a: 56)

There *is* a type of freedom to be had, nevertheless, once death and the absurd are recognized as given, the kind of liberated feeling experienced by somebody relieved of responsibility. Having accepted the limits of my life – the absurd and death – I can live it to the full. The emphasis on life's meaninglessness in the face of the inevitability of death is perhaps greater in Camus than any of the other writers considered here. However, it still remains within the bounds of Existential thought, since, like Heidegger and Sartre, he identifies the *temporal* element of 'existence' and this leads to his own formulation of 'mineness' within finitude: 'Assured of his temporally limited freedom, of his revolt devoid of future and of his mortal consciousness, he lives out his adventure within the span of his lifetime. That is his field, that is his action, which he shields from any judgement but his own' (64). Yet, as with Sartre, there does not appear to be anything in particular that can guide me as to what such a life might consist of. Camus refers the reader to the occupation of an actor, who, in the space of three hours, 'must experience and express a whole exceptional life', to which Camus concludes: 'In those three hours he travels the whole course of the dead-end path that the man in the audience takes a lifetime to cover' (75–6).

There is something very arbitrary in the sense of self and being here in Camus, for the actor may sometimes use in his life a gesture he has used in his acting, lifting a glass like Hamlet for instance, so that the difference between appearing and being is slight. Camus also points up the absurdity that the actor can live many lives, whereas we can only live one. However, at the same time, there is also a sense here that our lives are roles which we can adopt at will, rather like an actor, so that there is something arbitrary about the actual lives we would consciously choose to live, no reason to choose one life over another. And both Sartre and Camus would agree, at least in these earlier writings, that there is an equivalence between whatever people choose, whether it is to be 'great' or to remain unnoticed, to be a king or a beggar. For Camus, what sustains the absurd man is that there is a 'metaphysical honour' in continuing in a role, whether it be as a conqueror, a Don Juan or an actor, knowing in advance that he is defeated (86). And yet for both Camus and Sartre there is a privileging of the artist, the creator, the writer. As we have seen, at the end of *Nausea* Roquentin's project is to write the novel we have been reading; in Sartre's autobiography *Words* (1964) reading and writing are Sartre's life's project and looking back, somewhat wearily, he states: 'I have renounced my vocation, but I have not unfrocked myself. I still write. What else can I do?' (Sartre, 1964: 172). In *The Myth of Sisyphus*, acknowledging that the writer is no different in many respects from other absurd men, Camus nonetheless argues that 'creating is living doubly' (Camus, 2000a: 87). And towards the end of *The Myth of Sisyphus* Camus virtually comes round to a Sartrean view of writing as evidence of the life's 'project', that the works of the artist when taken as a whole reveal the experience and thought of the artist.

Despite Sartre's attempt in *Existentialism and Humanism* to put a positive spin on Existentialism, it is difficult to eradicate the impression in Sartre's body of Existentialist work that he presents a rather desperate outlook. Having identified a universe likewise devoid of intrinsic meaning or hope, Camus nevertheless ends his discussion of *The Myth of Sisyphus* in a positive mood. He envisages a Sisyphus who accepts his burden and 'concludes that all is well. This universe henceforth without a master seems to him neither sterile nor futile. . . . The struggle itself towards the heights is enough to fill a man's heart. One must imagine Sisyphus happy' (2000a: 111).

As noted, throughout *The Myth of Sisyphus* Camus stresses the need for the absurd man to cling to the truth that he must accept his burden and live without appeal. At the same time, there is an indication that Camus finds in the work of some Existentialist thinkers a falling away from this clarity, and a broader intimation that Existential thought itself is prone to 'the leap', the resolution of Existential anxiety that Camus identifies in Jaspers, Chestov and Kierkegaard. However, Camus's own distancing from Existentialism only appears to be away from that line of thought which Sartre identifies as Christian Existentialism. Camus's criticisms are not levelled at Sartre or Heidegger for instance, and perhaps are not applicable in this form, and in *The Rebel* Camus acknowledges that 'atheist existentialism', which might offer a way forward for the problems he is trying to work through, has yet to be defined (2000b: 215). With this idea in mind, that the absurd hero remains a happy Sisyphus whereas the (Christian) Existentialist has a tendency to make the illegitimate leap of faith, we can now take a look at Camus's novel *The Outsider*.

'The Outsider'

We might expect Camus's novel, written around the same time as *The Myth of Sisyphus*, to embody the ideas of the essay in the same way that *Nausea* 'lives out' *Being and Nothingness*. The fact is that the novel probably raises as many questions as it answers in relation to the essay, the absurd and Existentialism.

It centres on the character Meursault, a man who enjoys life in a free and easy manner. He likes going to the beach and being with his friends, and morality and sanctioned behaviour do not play any part in his outlook. Viewed from a traditional standpoint, Meursault is amoral and heartless. For instance, the book begins with his mother's funeral at which he fails to express any grief or any emotion at all. Later in the novel, his girlfriend Marie asks if he will marry her, to which he replies: 'I said I didn't mind; if she was keen on it, we'd get married. / Then she asked me again if I loved her. I replied, much as before, that her question meant nothing or next to nothing – but I supposed I didn't' (Camus, 1981: 48).

Everything changes one day when Meursault is on the beach with a couple of friends. One of them has had a fight with some Arabs and so they contemplate an act of revenge. It initially comes to nothing, since the Arabs disappear from the beach. Raymond and Meursault return to the bungalow they are using, but Meursault halts at the bottom of the steps leading up to it: 'To stay, or to make a move – it came to much the same' (62). For no particular reason, he returns to the beach where he finds that the Arabs have reappeared, and with no declared motivation he moves towards them:

> Every nerve in my body was a steel spring, and my grip closed on the revolver. The trigger gave, and the smooth underbelly of the butt jogged my palm. And so, with that crisp, whip-crack sound, it all began. I shook off my sweat and the clinging veil of light. I knew I'd shattered the balance of the day, the spacious calm of this beach on which I had been happy. But I fired four shots more into the inert body, on which they left no visible trace. And each successive shot was another loud, fateful rap on the door of my undoing. (1981, 64)

At Meursault's trial, much is made of the fact that he didn't cry at his mother's funeral, as if this behaviour is indicative of the heart and mind of a cold-blooded murderer. In the event, Meursault accepts his fate, and the book ends with him happily imagining the screams of a hostile crowd as he is about to be executed in a universe that is benignly indifferent (120).

The novel as a whole certainly presents a world where there is no intrinsic meaning, where, rather like Meursault standing at the bottom of the steps, to do one thing is the same as doing any other thing, to stay indoors or to murder are equivalent. To pretend any different, to follow societal conventions such as grieving at the death of a mother, is sheer hypocrisy if that is not the genuine emotion. Thus, we might say, Meursault remains 'true', sees the world and his place in the universe with clarity, and once in prison comes to the realization that we live a life without hope or appeal. More than that, Meursault at the end embraces his metaphysical condition in the manner of a happy Sisyphus.

But the novel is more curious than this, for there are features of it which do not, on the surface at least, fit with Existential or absurd thought, but raise other questions. Why does Meursault kill the Arab? We have seen how it exemplifies a world deemed to be absurd – in a world without meaning the character might just as well do this as scratch his nose (although one cannot help wondering if it would be the same for Meursault – and the same novel – if he had killed Marie, for instance, or a 'Westerner'). Also, it serves as a comment on Raskolnikov's actions in *Crime and Punishment*. There the character suffers psychologically both before and after his crime, as he struggles to transform himself into a Napoleon, into Nietzsche's *übermensch*, by acting beyond accepted law and morality. Meursault kills without reason and shows no conscience pangs. The distance travelled between the Existential angst of the murderer Raskolnikov, or Kierkegaard's would-be murderer Abraham for that matter, and the indifferent Meursault, is the difference within Existentialism between the overtly spiritual and the secular. It would seem that we have moved from a world where the individual is fully immersed in the concerns of the everyday and struggles to extract him- or herself from the realm of the they and assert or construct his or her authentic being, to a world which begins with indifference and ends with pariah status for the individualistic outsider. *The Outsider* is usually interpreted as one which shows a character at odds with society simply because he is prepared to adhere to the truth of his self. In this interpretation Meursault retains his integrity precisely because he will not pretend to emotions he does not experience: love for Marie, grief for his mother's death, remorse for the murder. His 'yea-saying' at the end of the novel would seem to move beyond this towards a Nietzschean acceptance of the world, especially within the context of condemnation of him by the mass of humanity; it is also Nietzschean, perhaps, in that he stays true to his own set of values. However, since the killing is unmotivated and is asked to be judged by the reader only in terms of Meursault's emotional honesty, it lacks the force of the murder as an intellectual act that we witness in Dostoevsky's *Crime and Punishment*. Having identified this ambivalence in the role of murder within *The Outsider*, as if the novel cannot quite decide what its symbolic import is, it is interesting to note that in Camus's next major work, it is the question of the right to murder that takes centre-stage.

'The Rebel'

In post-War France the issues of Communism, Marxism and Russia were very much the topics of the day. In this public cauldron 'Search for a Method' was Sartre's attempt to marry Existentialism with Marxism, to bring Being into History, to make self and situation equal forces. Camus also felt a necessity to bring his ideas on the absurd and the solitary individual up against explicit thinking from the Left; the result was *The Rebel*. It begins by noting that in the middle of the twentieth century the world has seen the death and upheaval of 70 million people. Once upon a time, murder was seen as an irrational act, a crime of passion. Heathcliff, for example, would have murdered for Cathy but would never have sought to justify it beyond saying that he loved her above all else (Camus, 2000b: 11). But the twentieth century has seen murder become 'reasonable': all murder can now be justified by logic.

If we think of the way murder is portrayed in *The Outsider*, it is a matter of indifference. Camus, without explicit reference to the novel, examines in *The Rebel* this same attitude. In an absurd universe, to kill would indeed seem to be a matter of indifference. Yet, if we think of murder through the notion of the absurd, as happens in *The Myth of Sisyphus*, Camus says that we are once more led to an absurd position. In *The Myth of Sisyphus* he argues that the absurd position with respect to the individual means that the only philosophically legitimate action one can take is to continue the encounter between life and a meaningless universe. Suicide might appear a means of escape, but in Camus's reckoning this is metaphysically inconsistent. There is a similar inconsistency if we attempt murder:

> Equally, if one denies that there are grounds for suicide, one cannot claim them for murder. One cannot be a part-time nihilist. Absurdist reasoning cannot defend the continued existence of its spokesman and accept the sacrifice of others' lives. The moment we recognize the impossibility of absolute negation (and living is a manner of recognizing this) the very first thing that cannot be denied is the right of others to live. Thus, the self-same notion which allowed us to think that murder was a matter of indifference now undermines its justifications; we are back in the untenable position from which we tried to escape. In practice, this line of reasoning tells us at one and the same time that killing is permissible and that it is not permissible. It abandons us in contradiction, with no grounds for forbidding murder or for justifying it, menacing and exposed to menace, driven by an entire world intoxicated with nihilism, and yet lost in loneliness, with knives in our hands and a lump in our throats. Nothing remains in the absurdist attitude which can help us answer the questions of our time. (2000b: 15–16)

Faced once again with the absurd, and knowing that suicide is not an answer, Camus proceeds to demonstrate how we can live in the midst of this paradox and in a time which demands that we act, for to do nothing is to condone murder, and yet, again paradoxically, it is shown that to act in the twentieth century is to kill. Camus demonstrates that it is the figure of the rebel alone who can continue the 'absurdist wager'. Apparently trapped in the cul-de-sac of thought when applied to murder and the absurd, Camus says that there is no ground from which to start except the original ground of rebellion, the simultaneous 'yes' and 'no' which runs through *The Myth* and ends *The Outsider*. In *The Myth* Camus asks for a 'permanent personal revolt'. This is exactly the figure of the rebel: 'I proclaim that I believe in nothing and that everything is absurd, but I cannot doubt the validity of my own proclamation and I am compelled to believe, at least, in my own protest' (2000b: 16). What is different in *The Rebel*, however, is that now Camus argues that this rebellion is a communal response to a universal condition rather than an individual one. It is no longer the solitary outsider figure, clinging to the truth of his or her subjective world, which provides the rock from which to build, but the shared rebellion of all those who suffer: 'Rebellion is the common ground on which every man bases his first values. I *rebel* – therefore we *exist*' (28).

In *The Rebel*, Camus explicitly moves on from the rank individualism of *The Myth of Sisyphus* and *The Outsider* to a social or communal sense of the metaphysical human condition. Whether this should be seen as a development of the earlier work or as a break from it is unclear, whereas Sartre's embrace of Marxism appears much less ambiguous as a sidelining of central Existential tenets.

However, as with Sartre, there are lines of argument which seem to continue directly from the earlier, more doggedly Existential work. One line of argument in *The Myth* and *The Rebel* which is often overlooked because it does not fit in with romantic notions of the outsider figure is the injunction to stay within limits. Camus says in *The Rebel* that 'Suicide and murder are thus two aspects of a single system, the system of an unhappy intellect which rather than suffer limitation chooses the dark victory which annihilates earth and heaven' (2000b: 15). Time and again in *The Rebel*, Camus returns to the idea that it is only by accepting the limits of the human situation, by sticking with what we know and can know, that we will avoid repeating the horrors of the twentieth century as witnessed to its midpoint, and actually preserve what may be beyond our ken. The argument is perfectly consistent with what he says in *The Myth*, and perhaps even *The Outsider*, since in the latter Meursault accepts his life as it has been lived and is about to be extinguished. According to Camus, the Final Solution of the Nazis is what happens when we do not accept living in paradox, living in the absurd: the Nazis attempted to impose themselves on the world in order that they might remove the paradox through annihilation. Similarly, the terror that is perpetrated by Russia at the time of Camus's writing is an attempt to impose something other than what is understood as the limits of the human situation. In *The Myth* Camus argues that there can be no freedom except the kind of freedom that comes from accepting the limits of the human situation: the absurd and impending death. *The Rebel* is consistent with this when it proposes 'moderation', an acceptance of the limits rather than ambition for absolutes such as absolute justice or absolute freedom, or 'history', or God.

This is once more to live existence as paradox. Camus illuminates the human situation by comparing the rebellion of the slave against his master with the rebellion of man against the universe: both feel frustration and injustice, and in rebelling, both instate what is valuable for themselves and for others. Beyond that, Camus notes that revolutions begin in rebellion, yet once they become established, as happened in France and Russia, those in power take up the role of masters and a new rebellion is required. Just as Sartre sees consciousness as eternally creating, Camus argues for constant rebellion as the means with which to preserve what is common to all men, and so the shared suffering of injustice suggests something essential to mankind.

To reach such a point leads us to ask the question of whether this has taken us beyond the putative bounds of Existentialism. In staying with 'the absurd', Camus follows up his previous work, and it could be said that while it always appears in *The Myth* and *The Rebel* that each man takes up the 'absurdist wager' independently and subjectively, the absurd as it is described in *The Rebel* is a universal human condition: 'We see that the affirmation implicit in each act of revolt is extended to something which transcends the individual insofar as it removes him from his supposed solitude and supplies him with reason to act' (2000b: 21), and further: 'An analysis of rebellion leads us to the suspicion that, contrary to the postulates of contemporary thought, a human nature does exist, as the Greeks believed' (22). Rebellion is forever being renewed as a guard against extremes such as the excesses of revolution and totalitarianism, but we now have what is surely a moral injunction on Camus's part, no matter how derived, and thus what amounts to a social theory, for ultimately Camus says: 'When he rebels, a man identifies himself with other men and, from this point of view, human solidarity is metaphysical' (22–3).

The movement of both Sartre and Camus towards a predominantly social theory which assimilates elements of Existentialism appears to indicate the end of Existentialist thought proper, historically at least, and with regard to two of its main thinkers. We can now look at how Existentialism treats certain key issues and see how these have fared beyond the main historical period of Existential activity.

PART TWO

THEMES

CHAPTER 7

INTRODUCTION TO PART TWO

The second part of this book discusses key themes in Existentialist thought. It also broadens out the discussion of Existentialism into a variety of related topics and is an opportunity to show how Existential ideas have been challenged and where some of these debates currently lie. Although Existentialism is, in philosophy at least, consigned to the history of philosophy, I would like this section to show how ideas developed within Existentialism might retain their pertinence within contemporary thought.

Being and Self

A distinction might be made between two kinds of Existentialism: one studies ontology, the structures of Being; and the other concentrates on psychology, through phenomenology and/or notions of identity. In the second kind, Existentialism offers a brand of psychology which regards 'the self' as a construct, certainly, but also understands that I make 'Steven Earnshaw' in a way which is readily understandable as a bundle of traits of varying constancy, even to the point of being free to create (or stay true to) an authentic self, which in turn stays true to a personal project which I am free to create or to discover. This version of Existentialism was (and probably still is) the basis of its popularity, and, I would argue, this is the version of Existentialism served up in popular, accessible texts such as Sartre's *Existentialism and Humanism* and de Beauvoir's *The Blood of Others*. The other type, 'ontological Existentialism', is the Existentialism of Heidegger's *Being and Time* and Sartre's *Being and Nothingness*. Here, 'Being' is virtually impersonal, and certainly not to be aligned with the psychological self of the ego. In Heidegger's work there is little confusion of the two types of thought. In Sartre, it is as if the two versions of Existentialism converge and diverge. An early clue is in his *The Transcendence of the Ego*, which at the end points up the fact that there is a psychological self, 'ego', which suffers, among other things, but that this is not the entity of interest in the phenomenological sense (Sartre, 2004d: 50–2). The latter identifies a region of being prior to the psychological ego which is what Heidegger and Sartre are interested in as ontology.

Phenomenology and Consciousness

If we start with 'self', we start with 'consciousness', the medium through which we 'know' or 'experience' the world and outside of which, according to Existentialism, there is nothing certain or objective, nothing that is not part of the structure of our consciousness, even if, in some versions of Existentialism, the Other in fact creates consciousness, or modifies its structure. As already suggested, some commentators argue that 'phenomenology' – the discipline defined by Husserl – holds the key to Existentialism as a philosophy which can be strictly defined within the parameters of philosophical discourse. This chapter looks at what Husserl conceived phenomenology to be and how it was subsequently taken up and modified by Heidegger and Sartre.

God and Nothingness

The history of Existentialism could be written as a response to the question of God, even where, in the Nietzschean strand, there is a clear rejection of the notion of God. How has this been played out in Existential literature? How can this be lived and lived with? Without God we appear to be faced with an essential nothingness – however conceived – and with a concomitant meaninglessness. Quite often a spiritual language continues to pervade Existentialism long after it asserts that is has expunged such ideas.

Freedom, Ethics and Commitment

With a line of thought which increasingly sought to remove God from consideration of Being and self, from ontology, and with the move towards identifying self-created purpose and meaning within the context of 'the project' or 'the situation', the question of how it is possible to 'commit' is crucial. Far from an abstract problem, the Existentialism of Sartre for many was at odds with his commitment to Marxism. The roots are in Kierkegaard's 'leap of faith'. How is it possible to reconcile 'freedom' with 'commitment'?

CHAPTER 8

BEING AND SELF

Kierkegaard

In moving from the aesthetical to the ethical, and then from the ethical to the religious, Kierkegaard is all the time concerned with the 'self'. It is because of the 'self' that these things matter in the first place. But what, exactly, is 'the self', in Kierkegaard's view, and how does this relate to the self in the rest of Existential thought?

It is not easy to state definitively what 'the self' is in Kierkegaard, but I will try to suggest different ways of understanding the term. Although what might be taken as a definitive statement of what constitutes 'self' in Kierkegaard appears in his work *The Sickness unto Death*, before attempting the task of explicating that particular definition I would like to shape an understanding of the Kierkegaardian self by briefly looking at how it might be understood in terms of his three existence-spheres. By doing so, I would like to show that Kierkegaard offers different ways of understanding 'self' which are not in themselves contradictory but highlight how Kierkegaard presents aspects of 'self' which can help lead us into later Existential understandings of the self.

The three existence-spheres might be regarded as relating to three different facets of the self, which, when taken together, are what the self is composed of. There is the 'sensuous' self, that is, the aesthetic. This side of life is one of 'immediacy', enjoyment with little care for others, living for the moment. Then there is what Kierkegaard calls the 'universal' self, what we might nowadays call the 'social self', and which relates to the ethical sphere. Here the emphasis is on the moral world, of conforming to the normalizing demands of society. Both of these facets of self are readily understandable, whether one agrees or not that the self can be divided in such a manner. Finally there is the religious self, the self that stands before God, what is called the 'theological self' in *The Sickness unto Death* (Kierkegaard, 2004b: 111). This is the part of self which relates directly to God.

But what is the 'religious' self? In *Either/Or* the self is composed of both the 'temporal' and the 'eternal'. The 'temporal' is what relates to this world, our earthly concerns, which would cover both the aesthetic sphere and the ethical sphere, lives of pleasure and social lives. The 'eternal', on the other hand, is that part of ourselves which relates to God. It is not 'material', that is, it does not have a 'physical' base. Instead it is 'spirit'. Again, it would seem that Kierkegaard's 'self' as mixture of the physical and the spiritual is just a version of the self understood as a composite of 'body and soul', or perhaps a tripartite structure of 'body, soul, spirit' or 'body, mind, spirit'.

What is inaccurate about the above explanation is that it suggests 'the self' is simply 'there', present or existing as a mixture of these elements at all times, even if subject to some modification in the details over an individual's lifetime, when what Kierkegaard stresses is that the 'self' is never fully present, or at least not until it stands before God and, as discussed previously, 'chooses itself' or 'receives itself'. Until that moment, the individual is deluded in believing that it is its 'self', or, in later Existential (secular) terminology, the self is living 'inauthentically'. The self, then, is not some static category composed of the aesthetic, the ethical and the religious, or some static category composed of the physical and the spiritual, it exists as a 'potential' to be realized, it is a 'project' that each individual has to will. In other words, the 'self' is not (wholly) aware of its 'self', cannot 'know' its 'self', it has to 'work' to achieve a state of self-actualization. Here is a fuller description of the moment mentioned above in *Either/Or* where the individual stands before God:

> So when all has become still around one, as solemn as a starlit night, when the soul is alone in the whole world, then there appears before one, not a distinguished man, but the eternal Power itself. The heavens part, as it were, and the I chooses itself – or rather, receives itself. Then has the soul beheld the loftiest sight that mortal eye can see and which never can be forgotten, then the personality receives the accolade of knighthood which ennobles it for an eternity. He does not become another man than he was before, but he becomes himself, consciousness is unified, and he

is himself. As an heir, even though he were heir to the treasure of all the world, nevertheless does not possess his property before he has come of age, so even the richest personality is nothing before he has chosen himself, and on the other hand even what one might call the poorest personality is everything when he has chosen himself; for the great thing is not to be this or that but to be oneself, and this everyone can be if he wills it. (1959: 181)

This self, although sometimes defined by Kierkegaard as nothing other than 'spirit', is 'infinitely concrete'. This 'new' self did not exist before, 'and yet it did exist, for it was in fact "himself"' (219).

While it may be difficult to comprehend Kierkegaard's conception of 'self' fully here, reliant as it is on a notion of freedom which yet somehow demands choosing the 'self' which alone can stand before God, a self which was always there in potential and which is to be 'accepted' or 'received' when the self stands before God, it is easy to see how it becomes transformed, in later Existential thought, into the 'authentic self', the absolute necessity 'to be oneself' over and above social and public morality and norms, regardless of the cost either to the habitualized self or society. This notion of 'choosing the self' – although really, as Kierkegaard immediately corrects it, this is 'accepting the self' – has been transformed within some strands of Existentialism to mean that it is possible for each individual to choose who or what they want to be. This is clearly not the case in Kierkegaard, and he warns against it both in *Either/Or* and in *The Sickness unto Death*. In Kierkegaard, each individual's self is already 'given', although the 'given' is a 'potential' within each individual – the self is there and it is not yet there.

The idea that the self is not a 'definite' or 'concrete' thing is further developed in *The Sickness unto Death*. While the concept that the self is potential rather than actual is maintained, a definition of self is asserted whereby self appears as a consciousness of self, where that self is a synthesis of three opposite terms:

The human being is spirit. But what is spirit? Spirit is the self. But what is the self? The self is a relation which relates to itself, or that in the relation which is its relating to itself. The self is not the relation but the relation's relating to itself. A human being is a synthesis of the infinite and the finite, of the temporal and the eternal, of freedom and necessity. In short a synthesis. A synthesis is a relation between two terms. Looked at in this way a human being is not yet a self. (2004b: 43)

Again, even though we have the components of the self more clearly identified, this time with respect to the synthesis of these three oppositions, Kierkegaard asserts that 'a human being is not yet a self'. The book thus retains the sense of self in *Either/Or* as an entity that exists in potential, struggling in different ways in different individuals to realize this potential and fully become the 'self'. In *The Sickness unto Death* the state of not having achieved this state is characterized as 'despair', which is 'a sickness of the spirit, of the self' (2004b: 43). The book then elaborates on how the self can be 'healthy' by achieving the correct balance in its synthesis of the opposites, and also identifies different types of despair which relate to different stages of an individual's 'self' awareness: one is unconscious of having a self at all; one is aware of having a self but does not want to be oneself; one is aware of having a self and wants to be oneself. It is this last version, what Kierkegaard denotes as 'defiance', which might appear puzzling, since it is close to the common Existential notion of being free to create or choose oneself. It should be remembered, however, that in Kierkegaard's view the self is only fully realized in the standing before God, and at that moment there is a letting go of the self before it is then 'received' by the self. To want to be oneself is evidence of a state of despair because it means the individual wishes to keep his self *for* himself, that is, he does not wish to 'hand over' his self to God – the only act whereby the self is fully realized – and thus 'defies' God. To want to be one's self truly is to stand before God and be 'transparent' both to God and to oneself.

Heidegger and Sartre

In *Being and Time* Heidegger tends to use the term 'self' to indicate the entity which I regard as 'me' and as such is not identical with Dasein. The way Heidegger conceives of it is that the 'who' of Dasein is 'self' (1995: 150ff.), as if Dasein is the more abstract entity and 'self' is the name we have to give to our experience of it. It proves most useful for Heidegger when he wishes to talk about authenticity and it is from here that our idea that each individual should strive for authenticity, for an authentic self, most directly derives.

Initially Heidegger talks of the 'self' in its 'averageness', its 'every-dayness'. This is how we encounter it, and this is what we are most likely to regard as our self. However: 'The Self of everyday Dasein is the *they-self*, which we distinguish from the *authentic Self* – that is, from the Self which has been taken hold of in its own way' (Heidegger, 1995: 167). In other words, it is precisely this everyday 'self' which is not our own, which is 'inauthentic', rather like the Kierkegaardian self before it is handed over to God to be received back. However, Heidegger's use of 'self' is not entirely consistent throughout *Being and Time*. For instance, it is not entirely clear how the 'they-self' and the 'authentic self' can be separated, since he argues that the authentic self is not detached from the they, or the they-self, but is instead a modification of it:

> *Authentic Being-one's-Self* does not rest upon an exceptional condition of the subject, a condition that has been detached from the 'they'; *it is rather an existentiell modification of the 'they' – of the 'they' as an essential existentiale*.
>
> But in that case there is ontologically a gap separating the self-sameness of the authentically existing Self from the identity of that 'I' which maintains itself throughout its manifold Experiences. (1995: 168)

Here it would seem that it is the 'I' which becomes most closely associated with the everyday, inauthentic, (they-)self. Heidegger attempts to drag the reader away from normal associations of the self with the psychological, everyday unreflective 'I', and reserves 'authenticity' for the less tangible, 'relational' notion of self as potential, future-oriented and self-creating. It is important to note that Heidegger argues the authentic self is *not* 'an exceptional condition of the subject', but must remain with the structure of 'Being-one's-self' which includes the 'they-self'.

Sartre is also at some pains to remove 'self' from the common psychological understanding of 'self' as an 'I':

> Thus from its first arising, consciousness by the pure nihilating movement of reflection makes itself *personal*; for what confers personal existence on a being is not the possession of an Ego – which is only the *sign* of the personality – but it is the fact that the being exists for itself as a presence to itself. (Satrre, 1995: 103)

For Sartre, then, in a circular fashion that echoes the 'reflecting–reflected' idea of Being, the 'self' is the recognition that the self exists, the 'I' noticing that there is an 'I', rather than the fact that it has some characteristics of a psychological entity such as the Ego or personality, which in this schema are either less 'essential' or simply not part of the ontology of Being. How possible is it, though, to expunge such an 'I', such a psychological self, from Being, and yet still retain a notion of an authentic self? Existential thinking would appear to suggest that it is only feasible at a highly abstract level and that the self/being must be understood alongside a psychological 'I'.

Literature and the Existential Self

Much literature that is regarded as Existential in orientation has at its centre the struggle for authenticity of the self, and the various ways in which this is manifest has led to an interesting array of narratives. Of course, the literature rarely aims to deliberately flesh out Heidegger's conceptualization of authentic self in a way which could be directly matched against *Being and Time*, for instance. However, for Existentialism we start from 'self', from 'the subjective', and this has meant that there has been a natural (happy) affinity between Existential philosophy and literature, particularly the novel, where the 'self' is more often than not dramatized. As Edith Kern says: 'According to modern existentialist thinkers, the paradox and absurdity of life can be more readily deduced from fundamental human situations portrayed in fiction than described in the logical language of philosophy which is our heritage' (1970: vii). It is no surprise, then, that there is much to discover in the exploration of the Existential 'self' within novels where we witness the 'self' transposed into 'real' or plausible situations. We are not here seeking to examine literary texts in order to discover a replay of fully formed Existential ideas, but to see how such understandings of 'self' and 'Being' fare when viewed less abstractly, when psychology and ontology collide.

One thing that literature does is to demonstrate the difficulties in living up to Existential notions of an authentic self. With Existentialism increasingly popular in different versions from the 1950s onwards, much literature was interested, as elsewhere, with notions of authenticity in the face of social conformity. This was often perceived, from the 1950s through to the 1970s, as the pressure to act out 'roles' in our everyday lives such that the 'real' self was never present, often with the result of mental breakdown. Since pitting the individual against society is a common pattern in the novel, so the degree to which such works can thus be said to be interested in Existential ideas is always open to question. While we should not expect literature to follow the terminology of Existential philosophy, as already mentioned, we should also be circumspect about finding Existentialism in every act of anti-heroic rebellion. A novel such as J. D. Salinger's *The Catcher in the Rye* (1951), for example, has a central character growing up and trying to define himself against a world which he regards as 'phoney'. It therefore does have themes of authenticity and alienation, but there is little more to add than to remark on these surface affinities with Existentialism.

On first appearances, Camus's novel *The Outsider* bears out his philosophical understanding and Existential credentials. Conventional behaviour and thought are alien to Meursault and he embraces his execution as a fitting end to his life. Yet the manner in which we get to the end of the novel is not entirely consistent with the philosophy as described in *The Myth of Sisyphus*. When looked at more closely, there are curious anomalies which make the novel much more than an uncomplicated mouthpiece either for *The Myth* or for Existentialism. For instance, we have mentioned how at his trial much is made of Meursault's non-display of grief at his mother's funeral, taken to be a demonstration of his heartlessness, of a cold and calculating personality. In Existential and Absurd terms, he is seen as being true to himself, not conforming to the they. Yet the novel invites a psychological explanation as well, which fits less comfortably with the Existential, or at least modifies it.

At the funeral of Meursault's mother, the sun and the heat of the day become a prominent feature: 'Wherever I looked I saw the same sun-drenched countryside, and the sky was so dazzling that I dared not raise my eyes' (Camus, 1981: 25). A little further on this leads to the nurse from his mother's home remarking about the heat: ' "If one goes too slowly, there's the risk of a heat-stroke. But, if one goes too fast, one perspires, and the cold air in the church gives one a chill." I saw her point; either way one was for it' (26). The next key moment in the novel is the murder itself, and again much is made of the heat. Deliberating at the bungalow they are using:

> The light seemed thudding in my head and I couldn't face the effort needed to go up the steps and make myself amiable to the

women. But the heat was so great that it was just as bad staying where I was, under that flood of blinding light falling from the sky. To stay, or to make a move – it came to much the same. After a moment I returned to the beach, and started walking. (1981: 62)

The acceptance that any decision is equal to any other mirrors the quip that 'either way one was for it'. The blame for his actions that lead directly to the murder is partly, even largely, attributed to the role of the sun: 'I knew it was a fool thing to do; I shouldn't get out of the sun by moving on a yard or so. But I took that step, just one step, forward. And then the Arab drew his knife and held it up towards me, athwart the sunlight'; 'I was conscious only of the cymbals of the sun clashing on my skull'. After the murder he says '[I] shook off my sweat and the clinging veil of light' (64).

The paralleling of the funeral and the murder through the description of heat, and through the futility, meaninglessness and arbitrariness of life, indicate an intimate connection between the death of Meursault's mother and his killing of the Arab. But the connection can only be accounted for psychologically, by arguing that the first event at a suppressed emotional level finds an outlet in the virtually random killing, as if he can balance up the death of his mother with someone else's. Of course, it does no such thing, and he immediately realizes he has upset the balance of the day and undone his life, such as it is. The way the murder is described, as well, completely devoid of inner motivation, is similar to the lack of emotional reaction to his mother's death, with the impression that the sun is not just an incidental feature, but might also represent a sublimation of emotion. This suggests that the psychology of self is hidden from the reader in preference for the philosophy of self, because upon closer examination the two are not complementary explanations. This, I would suggest, is a tension within Existential thought. From Husserl, through Heidegger and Sartre's philosophical works, and here again in Camus, all the discussion of an authentic self is seen as largely non-psychological but existing in a rather impersonal ontological realm which of necessity excludes the more common psychological understandings. It can be argued for in the philosophical works in such a manner, but within the novel it proves much harder to adhere to. This could be because the novel is trapped in the older psychology that Existential ontology is attempting to dispose of – even in Sartre's *Nausea* and *The Age of Reason* the characters are constructed psychologically in fairly traditional novelistic ways. Or it could be because in transposing Existential ideas into more 'real' situations, it becomes much harder to construe a phenomenological Existentialism which does not depend in some way on an 'I' understood at some level as an Ego, as a 'me' (although not necessarily in the Freudian sense). Nevertheless, Meursault remains an exemplar of Existential cool, unmoved by the hypocritical social conventions of the day, adhering to a higher, self-contained truth. The novel does demonstrate, however, the difficulty in prising apart commonly held psychological presumptions about the self from the way self is conceived Existentially.

If Sartre's literary works are perhaps not as radical in their execution of Existential ideas as his philosophical writing, Ralph Ellison's *Invisible Man* provides an interesting way into the possibility of portraying the self Existentially, although the novel is not itself primarily associated with Existentialism. Published in 1952 and rapidly established as a classic, it has a nameless black protagonist growing up in the racist American South. He eventually leaves his background and heads north to what he believes will be the land of opportunity and equality. There he becomes a civil-rights leader until he discovers he is being manipulated rather cynically by the movement he is spokesman for.

Throughout the novel he is forced to question his identity, not only who he is but also *what* he is. The novel not only raises the issues and ideas of a coming-of-age novel, but also poses ontological questions. It begins with the protagonist's Prologue where he identifies *why* he is invisible:

I am invisible, understand, simply because people refuse to see me. Like the bodiless heads you see sometimes in circus sideshows, it is as though I have been surrounded by mirrors of hard, distorting glass. When they approach me they see only my surroundings, themselves, or figments of their imagination – indeed, everything and anything except me. (Ellison, 1979: 7)

There is an interesting inversion of the Existential idea that we are aware of self because of others. Here there is an acknowledgement that this is so, but the problem is that others fail to fulfil this role, hence he struggles to have a self. Nor is it just one kind of invisibility. His skin colour makes him invisible to white people, but, as he also discovers, he is invisible to virtually all others as they make him in their own image. The novel establishes early on that the 'they' which affects his self and renders him invisible is not racism alone. Travelling on the bus north he becomes the object of a conversation between two war veterans:

> 'Man, who's this *they* you talking so much about?' said Crenshaw. The vet looked annoyed. 'They?' he said. 'They? Why, the same *they* we always mean, the white folks, authority, the gods, fate, circumstances – the force that pulls your strings until you refuse to be pulled any more. The big man who's never there, where you think he is.' (1979: 128)

The they is what refuses to recognize him as himself and yet at the same time what controls him. We have the perfect Existential scenario. How is it possible to be authentic under such circumstances?

As any reader of Existential literature will find, repeatedly, there is no satisfactory resolution or answer, by which is meant there is no resolution or answer applicable beyond this particular situation, a state of affairs wholly in keeping with the nature of what we have seen is an individual's 'project' or 'situation'. Whichever way the difficulties are resolved can only be right for that particular self. In *Invisible Man* the closing pages leave us with an image of the protagonist living underground, stealing electricity. The implication is that authenticity is impossible when living among the they; through the metaphor of invisibility Ellison bears out Heidegger's notion that at the very deepest level, ontologically, Dasein is constituted by the they. But the ending does not indicate that the protagonist has found authenticity. True, the lack of a name, of an identity, and the retreat into isolation do suggest a stripping away of all 'they' constructions in an attempt to reveal a more primordial sense of 'being', but the Invisible Man knows he must return above ground. For all he has ostensibly beaten the system (hence the stealing of electricity), there is one thing he cannot escape: 'In going underground, I whipped it all except the mind, the *mind*' (468). He understands that paring back to consciousness alone is not a viable mode of 'authenticity', he must live among the they, and so right at the end he makes what amounts to a leap of faith: 'Perhaps that's my greatest social crime, I've overstayed my hibernation, since there's a possibility that even an invisible man has a socially responsible role to play' (468).

Doris Lessing's *The Golden Notebook* (1962) is an equally extreme rendering of the complexities of self and self-constitution, and the book's dizzying undermining of any stable psychological or narrative cognition also suggests an ontological exploration. The 'heroine's' character is fragmented from the start such that she has no single 'self', no entity that can provide psychic unity for Being, or at least be the convenient term for it. Unable to maintain one 'self', she keeps four different notebooks representing different aspects of her self (or different selfs) as the only way to hold on to sanity, although at the same time this in itself suggests a mental breakdown. *The Golden Notebook* represents the ideal coming together of all the notebooks, a gathering in and connecting of all the selves or aspects of self.

Like *Invisible Man*, *The Golden Notebook* is also written in the context of intense political activity – here it is both Marxism and feminism. How is it possible to even begin to have a self when there are these pressures to give one's self over to the public, to the they? Lessing's Preface offers the means to a solution, a solution which has some similarities with the 'leap of faith' at the end of Ellison's novel. She notes how at the time of writing there was a pressure, as a left-leaning intellectual, to kowtow to an ideology that forced artists to describe the intensely inner lives of characters (workers). Indeed, Ellison's novel ends with its character planning to rejoin society and in his very last words, worriedly, he says: 'Who knows but that, on the lower frequencies, I speak for you?' (1979: 469). Less worried, Lessing's conclusion in her Preface is that 'the way to deal with the problem of "subjectivity"' is to see the individual 'as a microcosm and in this way to break through the personal, the subjective, making the personal general . . .' (Lessing, 1989: 13). *The Golden Notebook*, according to Lessing's Preface, argues that the inability of subjectivity to hold together as a self is because subjectivity promotes the illusion that each self is singular, knowable only to itself. At one stage the novel 'collapses' one character into another so that boundaries of subjectivity are completely dissolved. This would be the extreme version of the Invisible Man's re-entry and immersion into society, and possibly represents a different version of the state of affairs he should fear most again: invisibility. Between Ellison's novel and Lessing's there is clearly no accommodation that would satisfy Existential thought in its drive to authenticity, but then the philosophical theses do not necessarily subject their ideas to situations in the way that these and other novels do. Again, we might come back to Camus, who argues that any 'leap of faith' essentially involves the introduction of a *deus ex machina* to provide an escape route, a solution both *The Myth of Sisyphus* and *The Outsider* adamantly decline.

The Self Now

I have suggested in this chapter that it is never quite clear what the distinction between self and being is in Existentialist thought. The common understanding of self is that 'self' is understood as a psychological term which tends towards a psychic unity: 'I am Steven Earnshaw, and I know who I am to a greater or lesser extent, a product of my upbringing, gender, education, genes, experience, etc.' The Existential self, on the other hand, is one whereby my personal history is very much a product of my current 'situation', and how I construct my self and pursue that self that I am not yet. On balance, it would be fair to say that the Existential notion of self deliberately counters a notion of psychic stability by emphasizing that the struggle for authenticity is ultimately fruitless, unless, that is, it is conceived within the framework of a 'leap of faith'. Even here, with reference to a Christian Existentialism, it would seem that there is nothing but anguish, 'anxiety' or angst, such that any good Existentialist would be embarrassed to achieve something like a state of contentment and serenity. To achieve such a psychic unity would suggest the self-deceiving consolations of a psychological Ego as traditionally understood rather than the authentic self of Existential ontology: it would, in fact, suggest that the individual had achieved the impossible state of the 'in-itself-for-itself'. Compare the ending of *Crime and Punishment*, where Raskolnikov moves towards a resolution of 'self' via an acceptance of Sonia's Christian faith, and which consequently many readers find 'unbelievable', and the ending of *The Outsider*, which gives thanks to a life lived without compromise beneath the benign indifference of the universe and which appears largely in keeping with the rest of the novel and an absurd existence.

Looking at culture from the 1960s onwards, a period arguably defined as 'the postmodern', we can see that a new notion of 'the self' has emerged, which owes something to the Existential self, but does have significant differences. While both the Existential and the postmodern notions of self might agree that any movement towards psychic unity has something illusory or unachievable about it, the Existential self is still conceived of as unique and 'owned' by the individual. The postmodern self, however, is not individual in any of these ways, if at all. Instead, it is merely a 'subject', no more than the product of environment (however defined) and genetics (Earnshaw, 1995). There is a version of this postmodern subject, however, which would appear to derive from the Existential self. It is the self/subject understood purely as an act of self-will, where I might be superman one day and the world's most wanted criminal the next. However, the arbitrary nature of this goes against the Existential idea of authenticity, that there is something intrinsically 'mine' even as the self is in the process of becoming rather than fully present. Further, the postmodern idea that we are a sequence of selfs, or can choose different selfs as if we were choosing clothes from the wardrobe, leaves behind the key Existential understanding that the self is a relational term. To choose different selfs is still to believe implicitly that each self is a self-contained unity, a concrete whole rather than a relation. In addition, rather than seeing a fractured psyche as a problem, indicative in the Existential framework of the gap between the 'in-itself' and the 'for-itself', the postmodern self revels in its lack of a stable identity. The postmodern self is not one racked with angst but is happy in its freedom from the burden of having to achieve a psychic consistency.

On a strict critical and philosophical level, the Existential self has lost out to the postmodern self. The postmodern self is a simplified version of the Existential self: like the Existentialists it argues that the self is constituted rather than pre-given, but instead of a self-constitution derived from 'existence' itself, contemporary theory and criticism argue that individuals are 'subjects' assembled by a myriad of external forces over which the self has no control. The picture is further complicated because this critical–theoretical version is not that of popular culture, which has a tendency to see the self as a concrete entity vaguely located in a land between our bodies and our minds, and with the possibility that the self can always be improved (cosmetic surgery; therapy), or being 'lost' can then be 'found' in a more acceptable state. Yet another version of the self, identifiable in both critical–theoretical and popular forms, is that the self is a narrative, the story we tell ourselves of ourselves: the sum of personal events linked together in narrative patterns. This too lacks the focus Existentialism has on 'existence', on the astonishment at what existence is as a dynamic force experienced by a consciousness amid the absurdity of nothingness and superfluity. Against the current critical and popular notions of the self, the Existential conceptualization offers contemporary researchers, critics and readers a quite different way into how we might understand self and being, even if Existentialism itself never quite disentangles the two terms satisfactorily.

CHAPTER 9

PHENOMENOLOGY AND CONSCIOUSNESS

Phenomenology was a philosophical 'method' created by Edmund Husserl (1859–1938), intended to provide a science of the mind and consciousness, or, in his words, a 'science of Essential Being' (Husserl, 1969: 46). From its inception at the beginning of the twentieth century, it has been, and continues to be, widely influential in all branches of the humanities. Heidegger was a pupil of Husserl's and it is to Husserl that *Being and Time* is dedicated 'in friendship and admiration'. When Sartre first encountered the phenomenological 'method' he was immediately enamoured, as if this was exactly what he had been waiting for in order to advance his own thinking (Aronson, 2004: 28–9). The subtitle of *Being and Nothingness* is 'An Essay on Phenomenological Ontology'. With such an obvious impact on Heidegger and Sartre it would seem logical that the study of phenomenology should be central to any discussion of Existentialism, yet, as we will see, the implementation of phenomenology by Heidegger and Sartre is far from straightforward, and so its precise role in Existential thought is still a matter for debate. Hence I consider here 'phenomenology' as a special and problematic treatment of consciousness within 'Existentialism', while also considering, by way of *Being and Nothingness*, the broader topic of consciousness itself as separate from phenomenology.

Phenomenology

For Husserl, consciousness is always consciousness *of something*, that is, it is always directed towards an object. Consciousness is thus what is called 'intentional', it 'intends' the object ('posits' might be a more appropriate term), or, following on from Husserl's precursor, Franz Brentano, it is 'about' something (Husserl, 1969: 119–25).

'Intentionality' therefore distinguishes consciousness from that notion of consciousness whereby it is an entity which is 'empty', to be 'filled up' later with objects. For Husserl there is not something which is consciousness and then things are brought to it, as if it rumbles away in the background waiting for action; consciousness and the contents of consciousness are one and the same thing. In being directed towards the object, consciousness must be involved in 'meaning' in a way that enables the object to be understood. An 'object' can be anything brought to attention in consciousness – for example, the book I see in front of me, my belief that it will rain tomorrow, or my consideration of centaurs and unicorns. In other terminology, 'object' might be called the 'mental picture' in my mind or consciousness, where 'picture' is taken in this broadest sense of objects, as listed above.

What Husserl believed was possible with the phenomenological approach, the 'phenomenological reduction', was the ability to provide 'pure' descriptions of the contents of consciousness and in doing so uncover and describe the structure of consciousness such that this could happen. To effect this, Husserl asserted, it was necessary to 'bracket out' the world and suspend all preconceptions (*epoché*; 107ff.). These preconceptions about the way the world is most notably derive from science and psychology; for Husserl, these are the foundations which commonly support our understanding of the world. As such, they hinder our access to proper descriptions of the world as the world appears directly to (in) our consciousness. In Husserl's scheme, the contents of consciousness are termed *noemata*, and the mental act involved in consciousness is termed *noesis*.

There are some points which should be noted in relation to Husserl's phenomenology, since these may help us to understand how Heidegger and Sartre take up phenomenology and more sharply outline the differences, as well as trying to establish more firmly exactly what is special about Husserl's phenomenology.

For Husserl, all that we know of the world is through our experience of it, and this is what science concerns itself with. This is 'natural knowledge' in the sense that it is knowledge of nature. Each of us experiences the world primordially, through perception. Experience of the physical world is 'outer perception' and experience of our mental world is 'inner perception' or 'self-perception' (51). We empathically understand the world of others through their bodily behaviour. All of this, *including* what we would call cognitive behaviour, is part of the Real (world), or takes part in the Real. This is what science, including psychology, busies itself with, and this is what phenomenology does *not* do, it does not concern itself with 'the Real'. The phenomenological method removes all aspects of the psychological which place these facts in the real world, reducing the psychological phenomena to pure or 'transcendental' phenomena, and by so doing we get at the essence of phenomena. The way that the mind works in this schema is that there are bundles of sensations, *hyle*, which mental acts 'animate' in the process known as *noesis*. Noesis 'bestows sense' on the hyletic data, shapes them, transforms them, directs them towards the content, the *noema*, which provides the 'sense' or the 'meaning' of them. The noema is therefore the abstract concept. The shaped data in/of noesis will be 'satisfied' to a greater or lesser extent by the corresponding noema (246ff.).

From what has been said about Husserl's transcendental phenomenology, the following should be clear. Although Husserl insists on the non-real nature of the objects of consciousness, he does not deny the real world at all. Nor does he come under that kind of Idealism, following on from Berkeley, which says that 'to be is to be perceived'. In other words, Husserl is not sceptical about the real world: 'For me real objects are there, definite, more or less familiar, agreeing with what is actually perceived without being themselves perceived or even intuitively present' (101) – it is just that this is not what he is aiming at. He is not interested in 'facts', which are the province of all sciences, but in Being. He talks of consciousness, but wishes to identify a special phenomenological understanding which is not psychological but is rather to do with revealing 'essences', and these can be accessed using his 'bracketing' method which in effect removes the 'real' from the objects of consciousness. He does not regard 'others' as a problem: 'I understand immediately what they are sensing and thinking, the feelings that stir them, what they wish or will' (101).

Both Heidegger and Sartre freely adapt phenomenology for their own ends; they both openly acknowledge their debt to Husserl while making clear their points of departure. How precise and successful they are in disentangling their own ideas from those of Husserl is not the central issue here, although I mention in passing some points which might be disputed.

In Heidegger's Introduction to *The Basic Problems of Phenomenology* (1927) he demonstrates how he will use phenomenology to answer the question of Being. Heidegger's phenomenology will consist of three components: phenomenological reduction, construction and destruction. *First, there will be* 'Phenomenological reduction', which as we recognize, is a notion taken directly from Husserl as described above. However, Heidegger immediately distances his own use of the term from that of Husserl:

> *For Husserl* the phenomenological reduction, which he worked out for the first time expressly in the *Ideas Toward a Pure Phenomenology and Phenomenological Philosophy* (1913), is the method of leading phenomenological vision from the natural attitude of the human being whose life is involved in the world of things and persons back to the transcendental life of consciousness and its noetic-noematic experiences, in which objects are constituted as correlates of consciousness. *For us* phenomenological reduction means leading phenomenological vision back from the apprehension of a being, whatever may be the character of that apprehension, to the understanding of the being of this being (projecting upon the way it is unconcealed). (1982: 21)

A fundamental difference between Heidegger and Husserl is apparent in this first transformation of Husserlian phenomenology. Husserl leads the phenomenological investigator back to the processes of consciousness as uncovered in the disinterested (transcendental) subject. But for Heidegger, phenomenological reduction is the first means of getting back to his primary concern, of getting back to 'Being'. Heidegger then introduces two further terms of his own: construction and destruction ('de-construction'). If phenomenological reduction leads us in a rather negative manner away from beings towards Being, he says, this needs to be accompanied by an opposite movement, where we ourselves move *towards* Being, freely 'project' it and thus begin to construct it: 'This projecting of the antecedently given being upon its being and the structures of its being we call phenomenological construction' (22). Third, the way we are able to understand Being is historically determined because however we approach Being we will necessarily be using concepts derived from the history of philosophy, and these will affect how we ourselves can understand Being. It is not that this tradition is without value, but it must be made explicit, 'de-constructed down to the sources from which they were drawn' (22).

It is possible to see here how Heidegger moves away from the procedure of Husserlian phenomenology and replaces it with his own phenomenological method, mainly because, as we have seen, the primary philosophical question for Heidegger is the question of the meaning of Being, not the contents and structure of consciousness. It is the aspect of 'destruction' that Heidegger first focuses upon in *Being and Time* when he introduces his use of phenomenology, saying that phenomenology allows *Being and Time* to avoid having to draw upon the philosophical tradition of ontology, for phenomenology according to Heidegger does not define a subject-matter, only a method (1995: 50–1).

The attraction of phenomenology for Sartre was that it offered a methodology for consciousness to encounter self or consciousness, or, more precisely, to describe the contents of consciousness in a systematic way which could reveal the structure of Being. However, for Sartre, this consciousness is one which is necessarily engaged with the world, not bracketed out from it. Sartre's version of phenomenology therefore appears as a hybrid of Husserl and Heidegger. For Sartre, there is much more a sense of a 'lived' consciousness than in either Husserl or Heidegger's Dasein, even if Heidegger's method for getting at Dasein is through what is revealed in Dasein's 'everydayness'. Sartre treats phenomenology as a powerful tool which can reveal and understand all levels of experience and thought, and consequently take us to the structure of human being. Anything can be subjected to the phenomenological method: my apprehension of the pen in front of me, the consideration of a key moment in my life, the nature of love, the structure of consciousness. The importance of it for Sartre is that in achieving an accurate apprehension of a phenomenon (as I have paraphrased it), we appreciate its 'qualities', and by 'qualities' Sartre means that in apprehending the whole we apprehend the *thisness* of being:

> the yellow of the lemon is not a subjective mode of apprehending the lemon; it *is* the lemon. And it is not true either that the object X appears as the empty form which holds together disparate qualities. In fact the lemon is extended throughout its qualities, and each of its qualities is extended throughout each of the others. It is the sourness of the lemon which is yellow, it is the yellow of the lemon which is sour. . . . The fluidity, the tepidity, the bluish color, the undulating restlessness of the water in a pool

are given at one stroke, each quality through the others; and it is the total interpenetration which we call the *this*. (1995: 186)

This description, from *Being and Nothingness*, is the kind of description which abounds in his novel *Nausea*, and which is frequently attributed to parts of Proust's *Remembrance*. For David Lodge (2002), this kind of description is what writers, particularly novelists, have done brilliantly over the centuries, the evocation of the experience of *qualia*, the experience of the world's *thisness*. It is the experience of 'thisness' by consciousness which is what perhaps separates out discussions in certain parts of psychology and philosophy from those of neuroscience, for only the individual subject can describe what it is like to have *this* consciousness as experienced *by* this consciousness. The modification of Husserl's phenomenology into the 'Existential phenomenology' of Heidegger and Sartre, then, is a way of getting to the very heart of existence. It is not consciousness as such; it is how consciousness can apprehend being and/or self.

For David E. Cooper in *Existentialism*, the main point of disagreement between Heidegger and Sartre on the one side, and Husserl on the other, is in the way the 'ego' ('I' or 'self') is bracketed, for in Husserl, in order to achieve pure descriptions it is necessary to remove the subjective 'ego', precisely the self which is prey to all its subjective preconceptions about the world. Husserl argues that instead of the subjective ego, we should aim for the 'transcendental ego', a reference point from which to describe 'essences' and 'meanings' and 'objects' in a disinterested manner. For Heidegger and Sartre, this is not possible, for we are engaged in the world through our 'work' or 'praxis', there is the facticity of existence, the engaged nature of consciousness, the fact that the intentionality of consciousness is part of this already-encountered world, the fact that consciousness is already 'about' something. For Heidegger and Sartre, according to Cooper, meaning is always to be undertaken within the totality of the world, which remains 'beyond' a total 'surveyability' (1999: 52). Consciousness is not a self-enclosed entity for the Existentialists, it is with the world and others, and, as we have seen in *Being and Nothingness*, 'coming to consciousness' depends upon others.

Cooper points out that for two reasons the adoption of phenomenology by the Existentialists is doomed to failure. First, there could be no such thing as a 'transcendental ego', since whatever it could possibly be has been bracketed into nothing. By the same token, any Existentialist notion of a 'concrete' ego would need, in Husserl's scheme, to be bracketed out along with all other empirical objects. Second, Husserl's idea that the 'essences' we intuit are then 'fulfilled' ('satisfied') by objects in the world is anathema to Heidegger's and Sartre's argument that we come to knowledge of the world through our experience of the world (Cooper, 1999: 52–3). Husserl's aim is for phenomenology to provide pure descriptions of/from consciousness and of the structure of consciousness, whereas Sartre is interested more in the experience of consciousness, its relationship to Being and its role in the formation of self. In terms of the role of phenomenology in Existentialist thought, then, it can be regarded as providing both Sartre and Heidegger with a 'method' for their ontology, yet ultimately it is a means to an end – analysis of an Existential self and Being – which could (I would argue) be arrived at in other ways, and had been, in a sense, by thinkers such as Kierkegaard. One of the attractions for both Heidegger and Sartre was that Husserl was offering a 'science' of consciousness, a firm foundation for something that could otherwise be rather vague: Husserl's phenomenology was essential for their entry into discussion of self and Being, but far from an end in itself. We will return to Husserl, Sartre and consciousness after we have had a brief look at consciousness in the history of Existentialist thought.

Consciousness

Whereas self and Being have been central to our discussions, 'consciousness', which we might think of as having a similarly central status, features in a rather variable manner throughout the history of Existentialism. If we go back to Kierkegaard and Nietzsche, we see two opposing views. For Kierkegaard, consciousness is much more than mere reflection. Full self-consciousness, the self as it is 'becoming', is tantamount to self-realization:

> The most concrete content that consciousness can have is consciousness of itself, of the individual himself – not the pure self-consciousness, but the self-consciousness that is so concrete that no author, not even the one with the greatest power of description, has ever been able to describe a single such self-consciousness, although every single human being is such a one. This self-consciousness is not contemplation, for he who believes

this has not understood himself, because he sees that meanwhile he himself is in the process of becoming and consequently cannot be something completed for contemplation. This self-consciousness, therefore, is action, and this action is in turn inwardness, and whenever inwardness does not correspond to this consciousness, there is a form of the demonic as soon as the absence of inwardness expresses itself as anxiety about its acquisition. (1980:143)

The leap from this to Sartre's reflection on the in-itself and for-itself is very small indeed. Here, Kierkegaard equates consciousness when 'full' as a kind of absolute presence-to-self, beyond mere 'contemplation', as consciousness full of itself, of 'consciousness' fully grasped *by* consciousness, what is arguably configured by later writers as 'authenticity', or perhaps Sartre's 'in-itself-for-itself'. Yet there is the spectre of a continual falling away from this 'fullness' and a concomitant anxiety at not achieving 'concrete' consciousness. This is very much like Sartre's self in pursuit of its self. In this version of consciousness, then, as a particular strand in Existential thought, consciousness is not to be understood as it commonly is, as the mental state we have when we are awake or thinking, but as the very process of being when we take it upon ourselves to be aware of the question of Being.

Nietzsche, however, sees nothing special in consciousness at all. In the development of human beings, he argues that it is the most recent function and so is not fully developed, but rather it is weak (1974: 84), as we have seen: 'One thinks that it constitutes the *kernel* of man; what is abiding, eternal, ultimate, and most original in him. One takes consciousness for a determinate magnitude. One denies its growth and its intermittences. One takes it for the "unity of the organism" ' (85). The cause of its emergence, he argues, is the social need to communicate, and thus it belongs to the herd (297ff.), and we are foolish to believe it is a suitable organ from which to 'know' the world or ourselves (300). Nietzsche specifically guards against any method which we would call phenomenological, saying that to start from the 'facts of consciousness' is to do no more than to start with what we already know and are comfortable with (301). He agrees with Leibniz and claims that consciousness is an accidental property of experience 'and *not* its essential attribute' (305).

Sartre would beg to differ. If we return to the opening pages of *Being and Nothingness*, we find that the book takes as its starting point his understanding of Husserlian phenomenology. In reshaping it, Sartre is somewhat critical of Husserl. While drawing on phenomenology, he states that Husserl has been 'unfaithful' to his own insights, and in the process of modifying phenomenology to his own ends, on a couple of occasions Sartre suggests that Heidegger's term Dasein can readily (and should) be replaced with the term 'consciousness', as defined by Sartre. The question of Being should be reformulated in terms of consciousness: *consciousness is a being such that in its being, its being is in question in so far as this being implies a being other than itself* (1995: xxxviii).

Being and Nothingness begins with a declaration that contemporary philosophy has done away with dualisms and is now focused on the 'phenomenon'. This is a direct reference to the importance of Husserl and phenomenology in general, since it can be credited with breaking out of the Cartesian mind/body dualism. For Sartre, the reality or essence of an object or 'existent' is the sum of its 'appearances'. Its reality is not 'hidden' behind the appearance, it *is* the appearance. But what is the *being* of the phenomenon? It cannot be tied to a single appearance even if it is coextensive with it; it must go across all of its appearances, be what Sartre terms 'transphenomenal'. Sartre argues that Husserl's conceptualization of phenomenological reduction leads to the formulation *esse est percipi*, 'to be is to be perceived', a form of idealism that lacks solidity (although, as noted above, Husserl specifically rejects such a notion). We can see that Sartre's own notion of phenomenology and consciousness, in contrast, provides him with a 'solid being' (1995: xxvi). He turns to Husserl to explain that whereas what is 'perceived' (Husserl's *noemata*) is 'unreal', the process of knowing (Husserl's *noesis*) is the reality of the event: 'Consciousness is not a mode of particular knowledge which may be called an inner meaning or self-knowledge; it is the dimension of transphenomenal being in the subject' (xxvii). Sartre is very close here again to equating consciousness with being, although at other parts the identification is not quite so absolute. In Sartre, consciousness is both the tool for cognition and the phenomenon of being.

Consciousness or the Lived Body

It might strike the reader as odd that I have not devoted a separate chapter to 'the body', since surely any serious philosophy must have some reasonable analysis of 'the body'. The reason for it is that for

Existentialism 'the body', although obviously highlighted in this way as something that can be talked about, is not thought of as an entity distinct from Dasein or consciousness or being. To distinguish between a mind and a body, or between the mind and the world, to make the 'I think, therefore I am' of the mind a certainty and to doubt the body, would be to follow the Cartesian mind/body dualism. Sartre expresses the Existentialist viewpoint most succinctly in *Being and Nothingness* when he asserts that 'consciousness *exists* its body' (1995: 329). This is best understood by tracing the argument that leads Sartre to this particular formulation.

The problem, as Sartre describes it, is that when we talk of our bodies, we are confusing what we take to be our 'inner intuition' of our bodies, that is, our experience of our bodies through the senses, and through such things as pleasure and pain, with the information we have of bodies from other sources, clinical and biological descriptions of the body, for instance, which tell us of 'brains, glands, physical and chemical processes'. The mix-up, then, is that what I take to be my body is really a conflation of my sensations and external physical description. This is wrong, according to Sartre, since it in no way accords with the way that I actually experience my body (although even here 'live my body' would be a more accurate phrase) (303). Sartre asks us to consider 'seeing' and 'eye': '. . . I can not "see the seeing"' (304), a notion taken from August Comte: 'The eye can not see itself' (316). It is a similar problem to consciousness, for consciousness cannot stand outside consciousness, we are always 'in' consciousness. Yes, consciousness can reflect on itself as consciousness, just as the eye can see itself in the mirror, but this is not the experience of existing either through consciousness or through the body. Given that there is no Cartesian mind/body duality, much of what Sartre says about the body is a re-enforcement of what he says about consciousness. The main emphasis, other than to dissolve the Cartesian duality, is to point out that our senses are how we exist in the world:

> Thus it is the upsurge of the for-itself in the world which by the same stroke causes the world to exist as the totality of things and causes senses to exist as the objective mode in which the qualities of things are presented. What is fundamental is my relation to the world, and this relation at once defines the world and the senses according to the point of view which is adopted. (1995: 319)

It might be objected from all that has been said previously that here, however, in 'the body', is something that cannot be chosen. Yet if my body is crippled, Sartre argues, how I experience it or conceive of it is entirely down to me: 'This means that I choose the way in which I constitute my disability (as "unbearable," "humiliating," "to be hidden," "to be revealed to all," "an object of pride," "the justification for my failures," *etc.*). But this inapprehensible body is precisely the necessity that *there be a choice*' (328). Thus, it is of a piece that choice (freedom) extends to my body in the sense that 'how I live' is no different from 'how I live my body'.

Concluding Remarks

The interchangeability of 'consciousness', 'being' and Dasein indicates that consciousness is indeed central to Existential thought, even if its conceptualization is not systematically developed between thinkers. We have seen that in Kierkegaard full self-consciousness amounts to a realization of the subjective individual, and in Heidegger and Sartre consciousness is the focal point for discussions of Being/being, to the extent that on occasion Sartre sees them as equivalent. I think that this is more than just a question of terminology – how consciousness is formulated affects the way that being and self are conceptualized in Sartre, along with the manner in which that conceptualization is reached. It is not simply the transparent medium in which thought, reflection, projection take place, but is the thing itself, is 'being'. It is constituted differently in the thinkers, and I will end the chapter by returning first to Kierkegaard, showing how in *Philosophical Fragments* he makes consciousness central to being and to his particular manner of (anti-)philosophy, and finishing with a brief look at the current interest in consciousness and how it relates to Existential thought.

At the very end of *Philosophical Fragments*, in a section entitled 'What Is It To Doubt?', Kierkegaard tackles the issue of consciousness directly (1985: 166–72). Rather like Husserl and Sartre after him, Kierkegaard appears to use consciousness in two different senses, although they are presented as different aspects of the same entity. In the first sense, consciousness is that process which receives sensory input without being aware that it is doing so, consciousness is working or operating without being aware of itself as doing this, without being conscious of consciousness. Kierkegaard's term for this is 'immediacy' (something like Sartre's 'pre-reflective' or 'non-thetic' consciousness: 'The immediate consciousness which I have of perceiving does not permit me either to judge or to will or to be ashamed. It does not *know* my perception, does not *posit* it . . .' [Sartre, 1995: xxix]). In this sense of consciousness, for Kierkegaard, there is no discrimination, everything is as it is. We could say that everything is 'true', but equally, everything is 'untrue'; because everything in this aspect of consciousness is 'immediacy', there is no discriminatory function brought to bear. In the second sense, or aspect, consciousness is 'mediate', that is, it mediates the material before it, or 'in' it. In this sense, consciousness is (self-consciously) cognitive, it is aware of itself as consciousness and aware that what is present to it is not in an unmediated form, it is 'ideal', what we might better understand as a kind of mental representation, or mental picture; this is what Kierkegaard also calls 'language'. 'Ideality' when considered alone, or when not brought into contact with 'reality', has the same state as 'reality' ('immediacy') – the contents are just as true as they are false. It is only when 'reality' and 'ideality' are brought into relation with each other that things like 'true' and 'false' and 'possibility' appear.

Now Kierkegaard takes this further to say that although 'reality' and 'ideality' are constitutive of consciousness, consciousness is not brought into existence until these two categories are brought into relation with each other. Nor is it that when the two are brought into contact with each other, it is only then that reflection takes place. Reflection resides in 'ideality', since consciousness must *presuppose* reflection, and such reflection is neutral or disinterested. When 'reality' and 'ideality' are brought into contact, however, this is truly when consciousness exists, posited as a third term in Kierkegaard's definition: 'The categories of consciousness . . . are *trichotomous*, as language also demonstrates, for when I say, *I* am conscious of *this sensory impression*, I am expressing a triad' (1985: 169).

Kierkegaard highlights another feature of the triad ideality–reality–consciousness. Reflection is not in itself 'doubt'; doubt, in fact, resides in consciousness (or *is* consciousness) as a result of the relation between ideality and reality. For Kierkegaard, then, consciousness is to be equated with both doubt and interest. This conceptualization of consciousness as a restless questioning and engagement, a refusal to accept the idea that objective knowledge is possible as a higher 'expression' than that of subjective doubt, is typical of Existential thought:

Reflection is the possibility of the relation [between ideality and reality]. This can also be stated as follows: Reflection is *disinterested*. Consciousness, however, is the relation and thereby is interest, a duality that is perfectly and with pregnant double meaning expressed in the word 'interest' (*interesse* [being between]). Therefore, all disinterested knowledge (mathematics, esthetics, metaphysics) is only the presupposition of doubt. As soon as interest is canceled, doubt is not conquered but is neutralized, and all such knowledge is simply a retrogression. Thus it would be a misunderstanding for someone to think that doubt can be overcome by so-called objective thinking. Doubt is a higher form than any objective thinking, for it presupposes the latter but has something more, a third, which is interest or consciousness. (1985: 170)

We should not, therefore, be aiming to conquer doubt, since it is 'the beginning of the highest form of existence' (170), and this has been the mistake of philosophy, that its aim has been to create systems which remove all doubt. 'Interest' or Kierkegaardian 'consciousness', as described here, advance the idea of the individual whose real existence in the world is via consciousness that is already passionately interested in its existence, but which also continuously tries to deny this interest (doubt) by replacing it with one system of objectivity or another which it regards as higher than the interested individual. As we have seen, this attempt to flee the dynamic, freely self-constituting consciousness is a typical theme of Sartre's as well.

The Future of Consciousness

All of this might seem a long way removed from the current and significant interest in consciousness as an area of investigation. The huge advances made in brain imaging and understanding of brain physiology would appear to diminish the importance of thinking about consciousness in the way that Sartre and other Existentialists have done. Hence a book such as Ted Honderich's *On Consciousness* (2004) has no reference to Sartre, nor does a more broadly introductory textbook such as Susan Blackmore's *Consciousness* (2002). The interest in consciousness is not that of a subjective analysis where the *final* guarantor is the individual thinker but how what can be said about consciousness ultimately depends upon how it matches up with neuroscience.

However, I would speculate, there may yet be work done which would bring together the Existentialist views of self, being and consciousness and contemporary work in cognitive neuroscience. Mark Solms and Oliver Turnbull, for instance, in *The Brain and the Inner World* (2002), describe how there is an attempt to bring together neuroscience and subjective experience. For them this would revive Freud's original project, abandoned because the neuroscience at the time he began research, the1890s, was inadequate, whereas now we have many new powerful tools for studying the brain. For Solms and Turnbull, it is psychoanalysis which provides the primary model for understanding of subjective experience. They show that at some level there will always be an interpretation of what the brain/mind is which depends upon a philosophical world-view, and hence both disciplines – neuroscience and psychoanalysis – have much to learn from each other (Solms and Turnbull, 2002: e.g. 41–3; 45–6; 54–6). Again, this might seem unpromising for an updated discussion on consciousness with respect to Existentialism, which, as we have noted, tends to take an anti-Freudian view of consciousness. However, it is intriguing to see that Oliver Sacks ends his Foreword to *The Brain and the Inner World* by asking: 'What goes on in the creative mind/brain? What is the basis of the Kierkegaardian categories: the esthetic, the ethical, the comic, the religious? Will psychoanalysis and neuroanalysis, separately or conjoined, provide an understanding of these fundamental human states?' (xi–xii). Sacks is no doubt being mischievous in terming Kierkegaard's existence-spheres 'fundamental human states' – they are hardly regarded as such in the world of science – but a return to the field of consciousness as explored by Kierkegaard, Sartre and others, in the light of neuroscience, would certainly be an interesting new development for both fields.

CHAPTER 10

GOD AND NOTHINGNESS

And when we speak of 'abandonment' – a favourite word of Heidegger – we only mean to say that God does not exist, and that it is necessary to draw the consequence of his absence right to the end. (Sartre, 1973: 32–3)

Sartre, in his popular lecture at the end of the Second World War, 'Existentialism is a Humanism', spent much time defending the new philosophy against charges from Christians that Existentialism was a philosophy of despair, and that it had abandoned the world to a hopeless relativism where 'everything is permitted' (33). Sartre acknowledged that there were Existentialists who were also Christians (Jaspers and Marcel) but that he, like Heidegger, was an atheist, and that even if there were a God, this would make no difference to his central thesis that 'existence precedes essence' (26). Yet the idea of 'God', religious terminology and religious concepts feature heavily in Sartre's work. Sarah Richmond points out in her Preface to his early essay, *The Transcendence of the Ego*, that he resorts to both mystical and religious terminology to paper over gaps in his logic or understanding of his version of Husserlian phenomenology: he uses the word 'magical' to describe relations between 'me' and consciousness; where 'consciousness' itself is 'spontaneous', Sartre uses the term 'emanation', drawn from a theological vocabulary; the Ego is created *ex nihilo*, out of nothing, just as God is said to have created the universe (Sartre, 2004d: xxiii–xxiv). The pressure of the theological on Sartre's ontology is evident, for rather than simply assuming that God does not exist and developing his philosophy from there, he feels the need to prove it by logical argument at a number of points throughout *Being and*

Nothingness. For example: 'If being exists as over against God, it is its own support; it does not preserve the least trace of divine creation. In a word, even if it had been created, being-in-itself would be *inexplicable* in terms of creation; for it assumes its being beyond the creation' (1995: xl). On a couple of other occasions, he appears to argue against the logical possibility of God. For example, Sartre argues that to know 'me' or my being, God would have to have the same subjective experience of my being that I have, yet this depends upon not being the Other while also recognizing the Other. At the same time, of course, God would need to experience or be 'in' the Other, experiencing the Other in a subjective manner. For Sartre, this is logically impossible (232). In terms of understanding our 'totality', Sartre has a variation on this argument (God cannot be both inside and outside subjectivity) in that there can be no 'outside' of totality, not even for God (302).

It has also been noted that Heidegger's conception of Being in *Being and Time* can appear very similar to the biblical narrative of the Fall: 'Again and pre-eminently, the tonality is theological. It was as if Heidegger's whole diagnosis of inauthenticity amounted to a quasi-secular version of the doctrine of fallen man' (Steiner, 1978: 94). This theological line of thought in Existentialism – the idea that we are 'guilty' from the moment we are born or are in consciousness – is traceable from Kierkegaard onwards. In addition, Heidegger's notion that we should be 'astonished' by existence is easily assimilated into discussions of the spiritual, and the Heideggerian lexicon can be viewed as a spiritual response that attempts to modify and reject other spiritual terminology. Steiner goes as far as to say that 'God' can easily be substituted for 'Being' in Heidegger (147).

How, then, should the atheist–Existentialist properly view the absence of God in the world, how should the atheist–existentialist view man's 'abandonment'? Sartre tells us directly:

> The existentialist, on the contrary, finds it extremely embarrassing that God does not exist, for there disappears with Him all possibility of finding values in an intelligible heaven. There can no longer be any good *à priori*, since there is no infinite and perfect consciousness to think it. It is nowhere written that 'the good' exists, that one must be honest or must not lie, since we are now upon the plane where there are only men. Dostoievsky once wrote

'If God did not exist, everything would be permitted'; and that, for existentialism, is the starting point. (1973: 33)

While Sartre does not deal with how Christian Existentialists can square their religion with Existentialism, Camus, as we have seen, is under no illusion that Christianity and Existentialism have become bedfellows because Existentialism itself is always looking for a way of mollifying its world-view, such that Kierkegaard, Chestov and Jaspers 'escape' the bleak picture of man's absurd existence through the religious. Camus appears to accept and assert the godlessness of the universe without qualm, and one would expect that surely this would be the case for most thinkers in the atheist–Existential canon. To understand the depth of revulsion that a recognition of 'abandonment' entails for the nineteenth-century reader, and the reasons for it, here are three powerful passages that imagine the horror of a godless world. The first is from Kierkegaard:

If there were no eternal consciousness in a man, if at the bottom of everything there were only a wild ferment, a power that twisting in dark passions produced everything great or inconsequential; if an unfathomable, insatiable emptiness lay hid beneath everything, what then would life be but despair? (2003: 49)

Now, take away the 'eternal consciousness', that is, remove God, and you get some sense of the abyss that is opened up, an 'unfathomable, insatiable emptiness', for those who might once have believed. The following passage from Dostoevsky's *Crime and Punishment*, where Raskolnikov recounts a delirious dream, could be read as an extension of this passage:

He dreamt that the whole world was ravaged by an unknown and terrible plague that had spread across Europe from the depths of Asia. All except a few chosen ones were doomed to perish. New kinds of germs – microscopic creatures which lodged in the bodies of men – made their appearance. But these creatures were spirits endowed with reason and will. People who became infected with them at once became mad and violent. But never had people considered themselves as wise and as strong in their pursuit of truth as these plague-ridden people. Never had they thought their decisions, their scientific conclusions, and their moral convictions so unshakable or so incontestably right. Whole villages, whole towns and peoples became infected and went mad. They were in a state of constant alarm. They did not understand each other. Each of them believed that the truth only resided in him, and was miserable looking at the others, and smote his breast, wept, and wrung his hands. They did not know whom to put on trial or how to pass judgement; they could not agree what was good or what was evil. (1980: 555)

The common idea to both passages is that without God, man exists in a world that has no order. In Kierkegaard, without God, man is subject to passion and will without the guidance of any ruling force; in Dostoevsky, man is likewise the prey of these without realizing it, each believing himself to be absolutely right – each person a god, in fact. No doubt both writers are drawing on the visions of hell drawn up by Christianity and repeating them in their own ways and within their own frameworks of understanding. It is Nietzsche who draws upon the same cultural iconography in an equally powerful passage, but here he is jubilant at God's death and starts to envisage a possible, if still terrible, world, where there is no foundation for morality and only meaninglessness:

'Whither is God?' he cried; 'I will tell you. *We have killed him* – you and I. All of us are his murderers. But how did we do this? How could we drink up the sea? Who gave us the sponge to wipe away the entire horizon? What were we doing when we unchained this earth from its sun? Whither is it moving now? Whither are we moving? Away from all suns? Are we not plunging continually? Backward, sideward, forward, in all directions? Is there still any up or down? Are we not straying as through an infinite nothing? (1974: 181)

Without God, we are cast adrift into a universe where we lack any kind of guidance whatsoever. Nietzsche saw it as part of his task in history to prepare the world for a world without God. His is the moment in the history of philosophy recognized as the acceptance that God is dead. It would seem natural after such a break, traumatic as it might seem, that despite a few pangs, Existential thought would and could move on to develop an ontology that was free from reference to God. Moreover, from the later standpoints it might be expected that all vestiges of the religious would have been removed. The passage from Kierkegaard which hints that without God there is 'emptiness' might be interpreted both as 'meaninglessness' and 'nothingness', two concepts which feature heavily in Existential thought. Is it not possible to discuss a meaningless world without resort to questions about God? Let us look more closely at how theological ideas have translated themselves into Existential thought. Apart from the terminology, such as 'guilt', which has a direct correlative in Existentialism, and comparable terms such as 'authenticity', we will also find that God continually occurs directly as a 'limit' argument in discussions, such that 'even if God did exist', it would not affect the argument being presented, as if the thinkers are still worried that God could be smuggled in logically via the back door. An exploration of God, religion and Existentialism will also lead to discussion of 'commitment', which will be taken up in Chapter 11.

We have previously talked of a common theme of 'awakening' in Existentialism. How does this come about, how is Dasein, in Heidegger's view, 'called' to itself? (The term 'calling' in itself has obvious religious overtones.) For Heidegger there can be only two possible explanations – an external source, which would be God, or an inner source, some kind of psychological phenomenon. Heidegger does not consider the 'external' explanation, but focuses instead on the experience of 'uncanniness' of Dasein, the alienation from the voice of the 'they'. 'The caller' thus becomes 'the called' in this instance (1995: 323ff.). Yet if God gets no further mention at this point, what can be deemed vestiges of theology appear later at the end of the same section: 'All experiences and interpretations of the conscience are at one in that they make the "voice" of conscience speak somehow of "guilt" ' (325). If we consider that a notion of inherent 'guilt', following on from the Fall, is fundamentally a theological concept, then we appear to have it transposed from the theological realm to the Heideggerian ontological realm. It could be argued that 'guilt' is used here in a manner which bears no relation to 'guilt' in Christianity, but it is difficult to see how, if this is the case, 'guilt' would really become an issue at all. That is not to say that guilt must then be understood within a religious context, but to understand how it materializes in Existential thought it is necessary to make this connection. It is certainly possible to approach 'existence' without recourse to 'guilt', as does Camus, and still retain a notion of 'authenticity', but for the most part in Existentialism it retains this theological undertow.

In the brief passage above from *Fear and Trembling*, what Kierkegaard presents the reader with in a godless universe is the prospect of an emptiness hidden beneath everything, and which at the same time sucks everything into it insatiably. This is the 'nothingness' that must be the case if there is no God. We have already seen in Part One that 'nothingness' plays a major part in Heidegger and Sartre when they develop their ontologies. But what, precisely, is nothingness?

Nothingness

One of the difficulties here, in the midst of a godless world, is to conceptualize what 'nothingness' could be in any given scenario. Repeatedly it is pointed out that we can only conceive of 'nothingness' as a companion to 'something', so that 'nothingness' is always understood as some kind of entity, as opposed to a 'real' 'nothingness', which would be simply that, a nothingness that did not depend upon any kind of contrasting presence, the *nihil*. Such a conception of nothingness is arguably beyond human thought since we can have no experience of 'nothingness' that does not at the same time suggest that the nothingness 'is' because there is something lacking or absent: we can only conceive of a 'nothingness' before the 'big bang', for instance, by imagining the universe and then deleting it, so that it is in effect a nothingness dependent upon our initial conception of the universe. Put in a more formal way, this particular 'nothingness' ('no thingness') is really a 'no universe' rather than an absolute 'nothing'.

That aside, we are led to ask again Leibniz's question: 'Why is there something, rather than nothing?' Of course, one answer has always been that there is 'something' because there is God. If this answer is not accepted, then we are left staring once more at the fundamental metaphysical conundrum of why there is something in the first place, and at how we might conceive of nothingness. For Heidegger, when he brings 'nothing' into the discussion it is to claim that our anxiety is over 'nothing', and that it is this anxiety which reveals our state of Being-in-the-world. There is no definite object about which we are anxious, as there would be with the state of fear. This anxiety appears very close to the description of anxiety in Kierkegaard as a means of progressing from one existence-sphere to another. It is the central Existential notion that there is no essential thing at the heart of us – our upsurge into the world is on the back of nothing, it is underpinned or underwritten by nothing.

Sartre also understands anxiety as something produced by nothingness. However, as the title of Sartre's work suggests, 'nothingness' in Sartre's scheme plays a much bigger part than in Heidegger's in how he constructs his ontology. 'Freedom', after all, is the correlative of 'nothingness', a fact that plays right through Existentialism. I will discuss freedom below, but we should note that in Sartre 'nothingness' is brought into the world by being. He considers the 'naïve' question of what there was (in the world/universe) in the beginning. He argues that it cannot have been 'nothingness', since 'nothingness' is only conceived in terms of being, it depends upon being. Therefore, to attempt to regard 'nothingness' as something which pre-existed being (consciousness) is to be engaged in something meaningless, since 'nothingness' depends upon 'being' – 'being has a logical precedence over nothingness'. If being were to disappear, nothingness would disappear along with it, it would not be the case that 'non-being' reigned (Sartre, 1995: 16).

There are perhaps two ways of looking at this. The first is that it is a problem of semantics, that 'nothingness' can only be understood as one half of the pair something–nothing. That is true for *Being and Nothingness*, but only in a fairly trivial way. Sartre's fundamental point is that nothingness and being emerge together, that nothingness only comes into the world thanks to being, and being, simultaneously, is haunted by nothingness in the shape of non-being. Once again, this is the basis for man's freedom.

It is also worth noting, perhaps, that it is not only the conceptualizing of being and nothingness that has biblical echoes in Sartre, but the style can also resemble biblical language:

Man is the being through whom nothingness comes to the world. But this question immediately provokes another: What must man be in his being in order that through him nothingness may come to being?

Being can generate only being and if man is inclosed in this process of generation, only being will come out of him. (1995: 24)

Sartrean Existentialism overtly rejects God and religious concepts, although it clings to these in other ways in order to develop its own insights.

Freedom

In a famous chapter in Dostoevsky's *The Brothers Karamazov*, 'The Grand Inquisitor' (Dostoevksy, 2003: 322–44), Ivan tells his saintly brother Aloysha of a prose poem he imagines writing. It is set in Seville, Spain, at the time of the Inquisition, when a man appears who to all intents and purposes represents the promised Second Coming. The Grand Inquisitor immediately has him arrested and speaks to him in his cell. The man says nothing to the Inquisitor, so in effect all that we get are the Inquisitor's spoken thoughts on man's relation with God, or perhaps this is man calling God to account. The Inquisitor describes the human race as fickle, just as likely to fall at God's feet as to watch him burn at the stake. Who is to blame for this? It can only be God, because God made man free. In making man free, man had the choice to accept and love God openly. But he has waited so long for the Second Coming – 1500 years – that his freedom has been a burden and he has, instead, given it over to religious authority. Thus man has been unable to take upon himself God's gift of free will: 'Well, I think you ought to be aware that now, and particularly in the days we are currently living through, those people are even more certain than ever that they are completely free, and indeed they themselves have brought us their freedom and have laid it humbly at our feet' (328). The Grand Inquisitor goes on to say that they have consequently made man happy because they (the religious authorities) have taken this freedom upon themselves and man no longer has to worry about freedom, he needs only to do what he is commanded to do by the Church. He accuses God of having created man as a 'rebel' in his freedom, but asserts that because it is impossible for man to be a perpetual rebel, hence again man must give up his freedom to those who are prepared to make decisions for him, and give others 'the right to bind and loose' (328). The Inquisitor emphasizes his point: 'There is for man no preoccupation more constant or more nagging than, while in a condition of freedom, quickly to find someone to bow down before' (331). In addition to this version of religious inauthenticity, the Inquisitor describes man as a creature who, in wishing to disburden himself of freedom, wishes to do it together with others so that he is part of a '*community* of bowing-down', in other words, gives his freedom up to the crowd, the public, the they (331). The ending of the tale is far from ambiguous, however. The prisoner says nothing when the Inquisitor has finished speaking, but kisses the Inquisitor and then leaves, and while 'The kiss burns within his heart' the Inquisitor still 'remains with his former idea' (342), as if he is both right and wrong at the same time about God and freedom.

Sartre's play *The Flies* gives us another parable to do with the burden of freedom. Instead of 'God', Sartre gives us a non-Christian metaphysical equivalent in 'the gods' of Greek myth. The setting is Argos fifteen years after the death of Agamemnon at the hands of his wife Clytemnestra and her lover Aegisthus. The 'flies' have been sent by the gods to plague the town as a symbol and reminder of their guilt in the murder of Agamemnon, since they did nothing to prevent the murder. Orestes, who was thought to have been murdered when a young boy and who is the son of Clytemnestra and Agamemnon, enters the town incognito on the day when 'the Dead' are released. This is a ritual which allows the town to atone formally for its guilt and to reaffirm the authority of the king. This structuring of the people in relation to authority is identical to that described above in 'The Grand Inquisitor' chapter: the people hand over their freedom to an authority that consequently takes upon itself the burden of creating values, laws, ethics, etc. In return, the people are obliged to do whatever is asked of them by the king. It is also very much the slave–master morality of which Nietzsche speaks.

At the end of the play, when Orestes defies Zeus, the supreme ruler of gods and men, the argument is close to that of the prisoner and the Grand Inquisitor, although here Zeus is far from silent, proclaiming: 'Orestes, I created you, and I created all things.' As with 'The Grand Inquisitor', there is no denial of God's/the gods' existence, or the role of God/Zeus as man's creator. Instead, there is an accusation that man's rebellion against God/Zeus is a consequence of man being given the gift of freedom.

ZEUS: Impudent spawn! So I am not your king? Who, then, made you?
ORESTES: You. But you blundered; you should not have made me free.
ZEUS: I gave you freedom so that you might serve me.
ORESTES: Perhaps. But now it has turned against its giver. And neither you nor I can undo what has been done. (Sartre, 1981: 309)

It is interesting to see once again that 'freedom', even with the self-proclaimed atheist Sartre, is bound up with some notion of a deity, as if it can only have significance through a theological framework: 'Neither slave nor master. I *am* my freedom. No sooner had you created me than I ceased to be yours' (*ibid.*). Orestes accepts that this will lead to his exile, 'doomed to have no other law but mine' (310). Just as Sartre asserts that there is only a concept of 'nothingness' because there is 'being', it sometimes appears that there is only a concept of freedom in Sartrean Existentialism because there is the question of God, although by the time we get to *The Age of Reason* (1945), God does appear finally to have been expunged.

Kafka's *The Trial* presents perhaps a more thoroughgoing tussle with the aftermath of a godless world. There is no mention of 'God' or similar; in its place there is a greater sense of man being abandoned, but without any explanation for his finding himself thus free. In *Crime and Punishment*, *The Brothers Karamazov* and *The Flies*, freedom is God's gift. In *The Trial*, K. is awakened to his freedom, certainly searches for something that might be responsible for his freedom, but can find nothing except what he is prepared to take responsibility for himself. Hence *The Trial* finds K. attempting to discover from other people how responsible he is for his own life, how much 'interest' he should take in it. There is clearly no answer; it is something K. alone can decide, it is not to be found 'externally'. That the novel abounds with legal imagery and concepts makes for an interesting comparison with a passage from Kierkegaard's *The Concept of Anxiety*:

> Whoever learns to know his guilt only from the finite is lost in the finite, and finitely the question of whether a man is guilty cannot be determined except in an external, juridical, and most imperfect sense. Whoever learns to know his guilt only by analogy to judgments of the police court and the supreme court never really understands that he is guilty, for if a man is guilty, he is infinitely guilty. Therefore, if such an individuality who is educated only by finitude does not get a verdict from the police or a verdict by public opinion to the effect that he is guilty, he becomes of all men the most ridiculous and pitiful, a model of virtue who is a little better than most people but not quite so good as the parson. What help would such a man need in life? Why, almost before he dies he may retire to a collection of models. (1980: 161)

In Kierkegaard's view, 'guilt' is introduced into the world at the time of original sin. Correspondingly, in *The Trial*, K. is deemed 'guilty' from the moment he is arrested, or awakened to his 'existence'. For Kierkegaard, to understand guilt cannot be achieved by deeming it analogous to legal guilt, but only by taking it upon oneself and deciding from within. The parable of the doorkeeper, and K.'s ultimate failure, would seem to bear this out.

Humanism

In *Crime and Punishment*, Raskolnikov attempts to become a type of Nietzschean overman, transvaluing all values, a Napoleon. He fails, as he recognizes, and his guilt at the murders of the moneylender and her daughter – murders he instigated in order to prove his freedom from societal norms – is evidence of his inability to go beyond pre-existing morality. We have seen that for Dostoevsky, if everyone were to believe themselves a god, we would end up with a world as envisaged in Raskolnikov's delirious dream. There is surely a similarity with Kierkegaard's Abraham: what if, in actuality, each of us were to follow Abraham's example and be prepared to carry out the murder because we believed it was what God wished? But that would seem to replace Kierkegaard's intense spirituality, each man standing alone before God, with an incommensurable idea that in a godless world such a movement entails that we each become a god. There is a passage in Kierkegaard which perhaps goes further than anywhere else in his writings to suggest that the closer each individual comes to God, the closer he comes to being God-like. In the second section of *The Sickness unto Death*, there is a distinct sense of God existing within each individual, as the conception of that individual, for the narrator insists that God is 'internal', not something 'external'. Now this could just mean that in some particulars the self has elements of what constitutes the realm of God – the 'eternal', 'infinity' and 'possibility' – as Kierkegaard asserts all along: the closer the self comes to realizing its potential, the more aware it must be of itself, and therefore the self's conception of God must also be greater. It does suggest, however, how even at this point there might be a rather 'unholy' overlap between Kierkegaardian religious subjectivity and an atheistic Existentialism.

This, along with the actions of Raskolnikov and Kierkegaard's Abraham, appears as a rather extreme response to either a godless world or a world in which we should move absolutely subjectively and individually into a religious sphere. Is there not some less extreme way which could take into account a godless world, or a radically subjective one? Existentialism has sometimes been associated with humanism, a philosophical tradition whose premise is that the values we create are not dependent upon religious authority but upon our own values as humans. Emerging in the Renaissance, humanism proposes that humans should not rely upon religious authority, but that through the use of reason humans themselves can create a better world for themselves. Humanism also regards individuals as autonomous. Apart from the idea of a 'better world', this does not seem too far removed from Existentialism, and explains why Sartre's popular lecture can take as its cue Existentialism's relation to humanism. Although the English translation simply states 'Existentialism and Humanism', the French original asserts the compatibility of Existentialism and humanism in that 'Existentialism *is* a Humanism' (emphasis added).

In his lecture, Sartre accepts that he ridiculed humanism in his novel *Nausea*, but argues that he was only ridiculing one particular type of humanism, the idea that man is the 'end-in-itself', that we all share in man's achievements and progress and that 'we can ascribe value to man according to the most distinguished deeds of certain men' (1973: 54–5). For Sartre, this type of humanism is nonsense since, for the Existentialist, 'man is still to be determined'. However, in a second type of humanism, Sartre characterizes the philosophy as a belief that man is always reaching beyond himself, is 'self-surpassing': 'Man is all the time outside of himself: it is in projecting and losing himself beyond himself that he makes man to exist; and, on the other hand, it is by pursuing transcendent aims that he himself is able to exist' (55). This kind of transcendence Sartre declares is 'existential humanism'. Why Sartre should want to align Existentialism specifically with humanism is not clear, although perhaps he was keen to counter the charge that Existentialism was a philosophy of despair at a time, the end of the Second World War, when to accept such a charge would simply be too unwelcome. Whatever the reason, there is an undercurrent which perhaps does make sense: Sartre is looking for a way to stay true to Existentialism while at the same time providing a means of *positively* going beyond whatever the current situation happens to be. This will eventually be provided by his own engagement with Marxism. Yet even within *Existentialism and Humanism*, it is obvious that, logically speaking and against Sartre's own assertion that Existentialism *is* a humanism, there is no reason provided here why the Existentialist *should* adopt the humanist outlook, the humanist idea that progress is achievable for the human race through man's own efforts, that is, without recourse to God or religious authority. As with religion, if we take Camus's stance, the doctrine of progress could only be a comforting delusion in the face of the truth of our existence. Sartre's move to embrace the ideological left after the publication of *Being and Nothingness* has been seen in opposing ways: it is the 'leap of faith', the kind of qualitative movement that Kierkegaard talks of when advancing from one existence-sphere to another; it is the precise opposite, a betrayal of Existentialist concerns, relinquishing Existential freedom to the authority of Marxist doctrine; it is an example of Existential commitment. It is the latter which provides the theme of the next chapter.

CHAPTER 11

FREEDOM, ETHICS AND COMMITMENT

Mary Warnock signs off her Introduction to *Being and Nothingness* thus: 'And, as for Sartre himself, we must realize that he is no longer an existentialist at all' (Sartre, 1995: xviii) and cites his 1957 essay, 'The present situation of Existentialism' as marking the break. It is easy to see why Warnock comes to such a conclusion. In 'Search for a Method' (as it was subsequently reprinted), although Sartre attempts to marry Existentialism with Marxism, he now calls Existentialism an ideology, an 'enclave inside Marxism' (Sartre, 1968: xxxiv) and parasitical upon it (8). This would suggest that by the end of the 1950s he regarded Existentialism as unable by itself to lead to a deep understanding of human existence. Indeed, for Sartre to categorize Existentialism as an ideology is to make its significance primarily political rather than philosophical or psychological. Simultaneously, Sartre argues, philosophy will always have a class-based agenda, since for him at this point in his thinking philosophy is the way that 'the "rising" class becomes conscious of itself' (4). As noted at the end of the chapter on Sartre, the anguished drama of the intellectual wedded to metaphysical freedom stands in some conflict with freedoms that might have to be understood and fought for politically. The move to Marxism nevertheless in itself opened up, or 'made concrete', a particular feature of Existentialism that we have seen throughout this book: to exist is to choose; to choose is to make a leap of faith. The leap to Marxism could be defended in Existentialist terms as precisely the leap of faith that Existential thought from Kierkegaard onwards had talked about. That was Sartre's right (necessity) as a free entity, although it should be noted that in taking up Marxism, Sartre's argument is now that freedom does not actually exist since not everybody is free under capitalism (132–3). However, there is some consistency, if self-serving, with his previous Existential writing in his emphasis in 'Search for a Method' on Marxist praxis when he claims that: 'Every philosophy is practical, even the one which at first appears to be the most contemplative. Its method is a social and political weapon' (5), although of course this also must therefore mean that Existentialism has no special claim to being a practical philosophy, and it is more in keeping with the tenor of 'Search for a Method' and *Critique of Dialectical Reason* when, as if answering charges from committed Marxists that his first and foremost concern is a non-practical consciousness, he says: 'it is not enough that "consciousness think itself"; there must be *material* work and revolutionary *praxis*' (14) and he contextualizes the revival of Kierkegaard at the beginning of the twentieth century as the result of a bourgeoisie on the defensive (14–15). Alternatively, viewed in the more traditional Sartrean Existential way, the leap to Marxism could equally be regarded on its own terms as an example of 'bad faith', of merging into the 'they' by committing to something which demanded sacrifice of the self for the cause of the many. In this interpretation God is simply to be replaced with Marx, and so Sartre's supposed 'leap' is in reality nothing more than an abandonment of the 'striving' and 'becoming' that identifies the truly Existential. But if this is the case, does that not make every 'leap', every 'commitment', ultimately a suppression of the either/or of existence in favour of an external system that removes the burden of freedom from each individual? It would seem, then, that a commitment to anything other than the self must at the same time destroy freedom for the self (commitment is usually understood as a commitment to something other than just the self). Does Existentialism have a way of dealing with freedom and commitment such that choosing commitment does not involve negation of freedom, or are the terms irreconcilable?

Ethics

Existentialism does offer an understanding which is at once structural and non-dualistic in relation to freedom and commitment. In the Sartrean view, we are bound to other people by the fact that at one level our consciousnesses are revealed to us through the very recognition of other consciousnesses. Intrinsic, therefore, is a kind of social bond, or however one wants to formulate it, even if it is a bond which recognizes that 'hell is other people'. Nevertheless, this intrinsic, structural bond should not necessarily be interpreted as offering up a social 'we'. According to Danto, *Being and Nothingness* 'denies the possibility of a structure of a *we*, my consciousness always being *mine* even if, perhaps necessarily if, penetrated by awareness of others' (1991: 111).

The term that bridges the subjective and the social in Existentialism, and which colours all discussion of freedom and commitment, is 'ethics'. But this has actually always puzzled me – why, if I am completely free, should there be the suggestion that I need to take into account a morality which could only ever be given to me externally, that is, ethics surely only relate to a pre-given social system and social code, a constraint on my freedom that is not self-derived, even if I internalize and individualize it. To start talking about ethics would seem to run counter to all that we have said with respect to Existentialism. Camus warns us off ethics directly: 'There can be no question of holding forth on ethics. I have seen people behave badly with great morality and I note every day that integrity has no need of rules' (2000a: 64). We have seen that Raskolnikov attempts to forge his own set of values, and that Nietzsche's project in *Thus Spoke Zarathustra* is precisely for those who would be the overmen and transvalue all values as they see fit, and such a view of ethics and morality would seem to be central to any understanding of Existentialism.

It is interesting to note that Sartre promises his readers a book on ethics that would in effect complete the work done in *Being and Nothingness*. In its conclusion Sartre asks a series of related questions: 'And can one *live* this new aspect of being? In particular will freedom by taking itself for an end escape all *situation*? Or on the contrary, will it remain situated?' and finishes with: 'All these questions, which refer us to a pure and not an accessory reflection, can find their reply only on the ethical plane. We shall devote to them a future work' (1995: 628). For some, Sartre's book seventeen years later, *Critique of Dialectical Reason*, fulfils the function of the promised volume on ethics, although for others, as already noted, it represents a decisive break with Existentialism.

Kierkegaard makes a distinction in *Concluding Unscientific Postscript* between ethics and morals, and defines ethics in a way which fits more with a putative Existentialist viewpoint. For Kierkegaard the ethical is purely individual, a stage on life's way, and for each individual choice the ethicist must act ethically and be clear that each decision is ethical:

> Yet ethics and the ethical, by being the essential stronghold of individual existence, have an irrefutable claim upon every existing individual, an irrefutable claim of such a nature that whatever a person achieves in the world, even the most amazing thing, is nevertheless dubious if he himself has not been ethically clear when he chose and has not made his choice ethically clear to himself. (1992: 134)

This, however, is certainly not the same as acting in accordance with the 'world-historical' system of values, that is, a pre-ordained morality or ethics. For Kierkegaard, then, ethics is purely an individual, subjective affair, part of the movement towards the religious stage and deepening inwardness. Is this view shared by later thinkers? Given that the emergence of Existentialism coincided with the rise of totalitarianism and continued through and beyond the Second World War, it is no surprise that Existentialist writers felt a need to explain themselves in terms that took into account the broader social consequences, in contrast perhaps to Kierkegaard's more wholly subjective viewpoint.

Even as Sartre asks us at the end of *Being and Nothingness* to hang on a while for his ethics, in the same book he shows a wariness of ethics and indeed criticizes Heidegger for what he sees is an attempt to introduce an ethics through the notion that in recognizing our contingency we at once feel guilty. Sartre says that Heidegger is right to identify first of all that '[I am] A being which is not its own foundation, which qua being, could be other than it is to the extent that it does not account for its being', but then criticizes him for attaching guilt to this, which will lead to an unwarranted ethics based upon this ontology:

> This is that first intuition of our own contingency which Heidegger gives as the first motivation for the passage from the un-authentic to the authentic. There is restlessness, an appeal to the conscience . . ., a feeling of guilt. In truth Heidegger's description shows all too clearly his anxiety to establish an ontological foundation for an Ethics with which he claims not to be concerned, as also to reconcile his humanism with the religious

sense of the transcendent. The intuition of our contingency is not identical with a feeling of guilt. Nevertheless it is true that in our own apprehension of ourselves, we appear to ourselves as having the character of an unjustifiable fact. (1995: 80)

Again, in *Existentialism and Humanism*, Sartre warns us off the prospect of drawing up ethical guidelines. He presents his audience with the story of a pupil of his who has to choose between staying to look after his mother or joining the Free French Forces. Sartre takes the audience through various possible responses and finally brings his audience to the point where he can declare that, ultimately: 'No rule of general morality can show you what you ought to do' (1973: 38). This is consistent with Kierkegaard and with Existentialism as a whole, and would reconfirm what has been described throughout this book as the dominant Existentialist approach to ethics, that there is no 'ought' that can be derived from the 'is', that there can be no shared ethics or common ethical base *necessarily* derivable from an Existential ontology.

This might seem a rather severe interpretation of Existentialism and ethics. After all, in Heidegger's philosophy such terms as care and solicitude, Dasein's comportment towards the world (towards its Being-in-the-world and Being-in-the-world-with-Others) would suggest that, Sartre notwithstanding, Heidegger's ontology quite naturally comprises the ethical. But again it could be argued that this would be to distort the way in which Being and Dasein are ontologically as they are, and that this 'is' cannot lead to any 'ought'. Even if one were to try to derive an ethics from the Heidegger of *Being and Time*, such an attempt would have to overcome the fact that Dasein's realization of its own potentiality-for-Being is at the expense of the they-self, even as the they-self is part of its structure. Rather like Kierkegaard's Abraham and the singular standing before God of the self, each Dasein's confrontation with its own death is a unique meaning or significance for that particular Dasein: it is not translatable, communicable, societal or public.

Nevertheless, there *are* perhaps a couple of areas in Existential thought which can be regarded as providing an ethics, ideas that are fully in keeping with Existentialist thought and yet more broadly socially applicable. First, there is the idea that in choosing for myself I choose for all humanity, and therefore that I have an absolute responsibility for my actions that must respect one and all:

> When a man commits himself to anything, fully realising that he is not only choosing what he will be, but is thereby at the same time a legislator deciding for the whole of mankind – in such a moment a man cannot escape from the sense of complete and profound responsibility. . . . Certainly, many people think that in what they are doing they commit no-one but themselves to anything and if you ask them, 'What would happen if everyone did so?' they shrug their shoulders and reply, 'Everyone does not do so.' But in truth, one ought always to ask oneself what would happen if everyone did as one is doing; nor can one escape from that disturbing thought except by a kind of self-deception. The man who lies in self-excuse, by saying 'Everyone will not do it' must be ill at ease in his conscience, for the act of lying implies the universal value which it denies. (Sartre, 1973: 30–1)

> So every man ought to say, 'Am I really a man who has the right to act in such a manner that humanity regulates itself by what I do.' If a man does not say that, he is dissembling his anguish. (32)

Sartre delineates it in such a way that the ethical injunction is not something 'added on' to make Existentialism more socially acceptable, but is intrinsic to decision-making, although even here he is saying that if one does not ask oneself these questions, one 'ought' to. This move from the 'is' to the 'ought' is another reason why the Existentialism of *Existentialism and Humanism* can be regarded as different from the tenor of *Being and Nothingness*. Nevertheless, in *Existentialism and Humanism* Sartre does indeed find a precedent in Kierkegaard when he interprets Abraham's anguish, as relayed by Kierkegaard, as his awareness that his decision is made for all men (1973: 31). Yet there is perhaps a telling confusion in Sartre's idea that in choosing for one I choose for all. Does he mean the 'form' of the act, that is, it is choice itself as contingent upon freedom which I affirm for everybody when I choose in this way, or does he mean that in the actual choice I make (either stay with mother or join the Free French Forces) I should be happy to make such a choice for all, or that I should be happy if everybody faced with the same decision were to make the same choice? In the abstract sense, the notion that there is 'choice' is that there is choice for all, but in concrete particulars it would only be a matter of conscience that I would ask others to perform the same actions as I choose for myself, or be happy that they did so. Kierkegaard's formulation of Abraham's choice confines it to a matter of absolute subjectivity, and the narrator indeed makes a joke at the expense of those who might think to imitate Abraham's actions with a view to gaining God's favour. However, in a footnote in *Concluding Unscientific Postscript*, Kierkegaard suggests an ethical viewpoint which is close to Sartre's idea that in choosing for one I choose for all humanity, and that each person is ethically bound to be 'responsible for the use of his life' (1992: 343–4).

The second idea which can be construed as an ethics is Sartre's argument that it is in my interest to guarantee the freedom of others since this will guarantee my own freedom:

> in thus willing freedom, we discover that it depends entirely upon the freedom of others and that the freedom of others depends upon our own. Obviously, freedom as the definition of a man does not depend upon others, but as soon as there is a commitment, I am obliged to will the liberty of others at the same time as mine. (1973: 51–2)

But once again, rather than revealing the nature of freedom, he is taking freedom in two different ways. Ontologically, 'as the definition of man', it is confined to man and thus to the individual. It is only when commitment comes into the picture, and this is defined by Sartre in a way which is ethical, that the freedom of others is a necessity or moral obligation. It is worth noting that this second idea of freedom, which Sartre ties into an ethics, again is only present in *Existentialism and Humanism*. In *Being and Nothingness* freedom is an entirely ontological concern, and when discussed in relation to others is seen problematically as a negative dependency and constraint upon my ability to be authentic. Again, unpalatable as it may be, to argue that individuals, in the nature of an ethical obligation, *must* will or guarantee each other's freedom at the same time as they will their own is not derivable of necessity from Sartre's ontology; he could, after all, take the Nietzschean (and perhaps more consistent) line that at this level as well it is a matter for individual valuation and transvaluation.

Again, nevertheless, while Sartre's argument on mutual guarantees of freedom is to be found in *Existentialism and Humanism* but not in *Being and Nothingness*, there is a similar (if untypical) idea to be found in Kierkegaard: 'The most resigned a human being can be is to acknowledge the given independence in every human being and to the best of one's ability do everything in order truly to help someone retain it' (1992: 260). If there is an ethics that is embedded within Existentialism's ontology then it is perhaps along these lines where there is a structural necessity for a freedom which guarantees everybody's freedom. It can be seen that this easily slides over into the more commonly regarded notion of ethical behaviour which manifests itself in declarations for individual, social, political and cultural freedoms.

Simone de Beauvoir, in her novel *The Blood of Others* (1945) and in her book *The Ethics of Ambiguity* (1947), dramatizes the relationship between self, others, freedom and ethics. The epigram to the novel is taken from Dostoevsky: 'Each of us is responsible for everything and to every human being'. It is quoted within the novel by Blomart, the main character, over his role as a leader within the French Resistance (de Beauvoir, 1976: 122) and the question of what right he has to make decisions that affect the lives of others. As in *The Ethics of Ambiguity*, the suggestion is that we cannot resolve these issues, but should embrace the ambiguity that is at the root of our existence, not in a way which would be a negative acceptance of despair and absurdity (an accusation she notes that had been levelled at Sartre [de Beauvoir, 1996: 11, 15]), but positively so that we take ourselves out of the futility of a desire to make the for-itself coincide with the in-itself. I would suggest that the ambiguity she discerns is not too far removed from Kierkegaard's paradox, that we are a mix of the eternal and the contingent, and that this entails that we must live through all the contradictions. In *The Blood of Others* the main contradiction is that to exist is to be free, yet to exist is to act, and to act is to impinge on the freedom of others. The point is sharply dramatized because the situation that the characters find themselves in means that they must choose how to respond to the war and that any choice they make must lead to 'the blood of others', whether this be the policy of appeasement as initially pursued by the Allies (1976: 131), or whether it is to accept becoming a leader in the Resistance, knowing that one's decisions will inevitably at some point lead to the death of others, as Blomart comes to see himself responsible for his lover Hélène's death. The novel does at the end provide a way out of the ambiguity of 'the blood of others', the necessity to choose in the knowledge that this affects the ability of others to choose, as well as the ambiguity of freedom/commitment we have discussed so far. We are given Blomart's thoughts as he looks on Hélène's dead body:

> Those who will be shot tomorrow have not chosen; I am the rock that crushes them; I shall not escape the curse; for ever I shall be to them another being, for ever I shall be to them the blind force of fate, for ever separated from them. But if only I dedicate myself to defend that supreme good, which makes innocent and vain all the stones and the rocks, that good which saves each man from all the others and from myself – Freedom – then my passion will not have been in vain. You have not given me peace; but why should I desire peace? You have given me the courage to accept for ever the risk and the anguish, to bear my crimes and my guilt which will rend me eternally. There is no other way. (1976: 240)

We must accept all the ambiguities of existence, and if we are to commit to anything, it is to fight for the very freedom that guarantees these ambiguities.

What this might mean is briefly made explicit in *The Second Sex*, where de Beauvoir states that what she is attempting in the book is from the perspective of 'an existentialist ethics' (1997: 28–9). The passage reiterates the urge for an ethics based on Existentialist ideas, yet at the same time highlights the difficulties of deriving an 'ought' from the Existential 'is':

> There is no justification for present existence other than its expansion into an indefinitely open future. Every time transcendence falls back into immanence, stagnation, there is a degradation of existence into the *'en-soi'* – the brutish life of subjection to given conditions – and of liberty into constraint and contingence. This downfall represents a moral fault if the subject consents to it; if it is inflicted upon him, it spells frustration and oppression. In both cases it is an absolute evil. Every individual concerned to justify his existence feels that his existence involves an undefined need to transcend himself, to engage in freely chosen projects. (1997: 28–9)

The 'is' of existence is the 'indefinitely open future' and the ability to 'engage in freely chosen projects'; on the inauthentic side it is the subject's fault if he or she consents to an existence that is degrading. However, de Beauvoir argues, such degradation might be imposed from outside and she uses the rather un-Existentialist category of 'evil' to describe such a state of affairs. Sartrean Existentialism would not concede that we were the victims of others' actions in this way, for even though we are always situated, how we are oriented within the situation is up to us to choose freely. Hence Sartre can argue that if I find myself conscripted into the army, it is I myself who have chosen this state of affairs, I have in fact chosen the war, since I could choose to do otherwise, or be otherwise (1995: 555). The point here is not to show de Beauvoir as unfaithful to Existentialist precepts, but rather to show that as soon as there is an attempt to extend Existentialism into the realm of an ethics that can be considered 'social', problems arise, and partly because the main tomes of Existentialism themselves have little to offer in the realm of an ethics that of necessity is derived from an Existential ontology. As Heidegger succinctly puts it in passing in his 'Letter on Humanism': 'What is said in *Being and Time* (1927), sections 27 and 35, about the "they" in no way means to furnish an incidental contribution to sociology' (2004: 221). For some thinkers, such as Emmanuel Levinas, the focus on ontology by Existentialism is at the expense of 'exteriority' and of ethics. Levinas's portrayal of Sartre's view of freedom is that freedom is its own justification, but for Levinas 'freedom' cannot in itself underwrite freedom, since this embodies the kind of arbitrariness and irrationality which allows for 'murder'. For Levinas, rather than being a threat to my self and my freedom, the 'face of the Other' leads me to question my own freedom and demands that I justify freedom in ways not dependent upon freedom itself (1996: 303).

There are at least two other ways of understanding the relationship between freedom, commitment and ethics. Although in *Concluding Unscientific Postscript*, as discussed above, the argument is that ethics is a purely subjective affair, the ethical stage in Kierkegaard's schema elsewhere would suggest that the ethical is more in keeping with the idea that it represents the individual's relationship with society's mores, hence the ethical is often represented by the question of marriage. Here, Kierkegaard has characters represent the importance of the ethical in intersubjective relations. The leap to the ethical from the aesthetical thus does not signal the end of the either/or, nor is it the end of the aesthetic. The leap of faith transfigures the previous stage and incorporates it in some way into the new existence-sphere, so that the aesthetical is retained in the ethical, although transformed, and again, when the leap is made to the religious, the ethical is retained in the religious, although transformed. That is acceptable, perhaps, when the 'stages on life's way' are in the particular direction of increasing inwardness and movement towards God, but what role is there for this in atheistic Existentialism? When the question of whether the free individual should marry is raised in Sartre's *The Age of Reason* – should Mathieu commit to Marcelle? – it is blatantly portrayed as a commitment tantamount to relinquishing freedom. In Milan Kundera's *The Unbearable Lightness of Being* (1984) the paradox of freedom – again represented by the refusal to commit to a single other – is that it fails to satisfy any sense of 'being'; it produces only 'lightness', since we are tied to 'nothing'.

Nevertheless, the atheistic–Existential emphasis is on 'doing', at least in the Sartrean line. To exist is to be engaged in the world, and such engagement is how being is made manifest. Throughout *Being and Nothingness* the reader is reminded that a person is judged on the totality of his or her life, so that Proust is not awarded the title of 'genius' because of the works he might have written, but because of those things he did achieve. Sartre and other Existentialists who were politically committed stress that action, engagement, is integral to becoming. This way of perceiving 'engagement' can be contrasted with Heidegger, for in his response to *Existentialism and Humanism* in 'Letter on Humanism' Heidegger rejects 'thinking' solely as the precursor to 'making' and 'doing', to involvement with 'beings', and recommends 'thought' as the location for engagement with 'Being' (2004: 217–18). The Sartrean version makes more sense in its adherence to the precepts of Existential thought, since Existentialism is always aware that being-in-the-world is necessarily being-in-the-world-with-others, and the tension or ambiguity of this with respect to authenticity and the inauthentic or bad faith is sharpened in the Sartrean version. But what, in the end, is an Existentialist committed to, other than God or a political creed, both of which can be seen as examples of bad faith? Are there other commitments which do not attract such opprobrium?

Others

I have emphasized that Existentialism starts from the self, from the subjective, even where part of that acknowledgement is that we are intersubjective in some form or other, whether it is a recoil from Kierkegaard's public or Nietzsche's herd, whether it is Sartre's being-for-others or Heidegger's being-in-the-world-with-others. But there is another line of thought, sometimes associated directly with Existentialism and sometimes regarded as a departure from it, which perhaps offers rather more in the way of the intersubjective. Martin Buber's *I and Thou* (1923), for instance, is often listed in the catalogue of Existential texts. This work is in the form of a 'poem' which suggests two modes of being, the 'I-Thou' and the 'I-It'. For Buber, to say 'I' is always to declare one or other of the relations, either the relation of openness to the Other (I-Thou), or that of objectification of what is external (I-It). The fact that for Buber 'I' is always relational – with authentic being the I-Thou – would certainly offer a commitment to what elsewhere is termed the 'Other'. Buber's notion is that we are 'called to account' by the 'face of the Other' (and see Levinas above). Rather than the ontological neutrality, in ethical terms, of Sartre's notion that we are brought to consciousness (or awareness) through others, Buber's ontology, if it can be called that, is ethical from the outset. Sartre's being-for-others means that our being is taken for an object by others; Buber's I-Thou suggests that there is a being-for-others which means our existence is responsible for others. Authenticity then depends on intersubjectivity, rather than the refusal of or struggle against the Other, and the tension in Buber's scheme is to avoid falling into the I-It, since this too can be the relation we hold with others, or, more strictly, the (a) relation declared when I say 'I'. The fact that it is in the form of a poem puts it in the tradition of Kierkegaard, bringing the reader to 'the truth' indirectly, since it cannot be communicated by dictat.

Commitment to others as an ethical injunction, rather than simply the necessity to recognize self in the midst of others as an ontological given, is apparent in Saul Bellow's novel *The Victim* (1947), an early Bellow work which has an interesting Existential thematic but with a sensibility which is more in keeping with Buber than Sartre. Leventhal, the central character, is a man wrapped up in himself and his own concerns. His 'awakening' occurs when Allbee, an acquaintance from his past, turns up and accuses him of ruining his life. Leventhal initially refuses to accept that he has any responsibility for Allbee, but is forced to confront his own manner of existence, a move from the I-It to the I-Thou. This aspect of the novel is first established in one of the epigrams, a tale from a *Thousand and One Nights*. A merchant throws away a date stone and is immediately accused by an Ifrit (a type of genie) of killing his son with the stone. The question the novel then poses, rather like the dilemma posed in de Beauvoir's *The Blood of Others*, is how are we to act knowing that our actions affect others? In Bellow's novel, the actions which have such large consequences appear fairly innocuous: the merchant's throwing of the stone; a casual comment by Leventhal which costs Allbee his job opportunity. The second epigram to *The Victim*, from de Quincey's *The Pains of Opium*, suggests Buber rather than de Beauvoir as the foundational understanding for existence: 'Be that as it may, now it was that upon the rocking waters of the ocean the human face began to reveal itself; the sea appeared paved with innumerable faces, upturned to the heavens; faces, imploring, wrathful, despairing; faces that surged upward by thousands, by myriads, by genera- tions . . .' This again is the 'calling to account' which existence entails and which can certainly be taken as one ethical version of Existential thought.

Writing, Philosophy, Existence

At the end of *Invisible Man* the hero/anti-hero says: 'So why do I write, torturing myself to put it down? Because in spite of myself I've learned some things. Without the possibility of action, all knowledge comes to one labelled "file and forget", and I can neither file nor forget' (Ellison, 1979: 467). His withdrawal from the world of the 'they' is to be temporary: to exist is to act. And action in this moment consists of writing. It is a conclusion that Sartre himself often seems to offer. His autobiography is called *Words* and his *raison d'être* would seem to be 'writing'; in the collection of essays *What is Literature?* it is writing that is first and foremost Sartre's 'doing' in the world; at the end of *Nausea*, the decisive action, the 'leap' for Roquentin, is to write a book. The commitment in all cases is to writing. But, as so often with Sartre, this is not unequivocal. In his play *Dirty Hands*, Hugo's role before putting himself forward to kill the Party traitor Hœrderer is to write for a Party paper, and while this is regarded by others as real work that involves danger, for Hugo it is an evasion of real action.

Writing is perhaps an obvious commitment from writers, and likewise the commitment to philosophy, and to thinking 'existentially'. Taking it further, however, Appignanesi notes an interesting thread on the question of vocation in Husserl, Heidegger and Sartre:

> Husserl reflected intensely on that life problem of vocation in philosophy. What is vocation? It used to mean a call to the priesthood, a 'profession' of faith. For the philosopher, it is a call to heedfulness but unprofessed unless he calls *others* to heedfulness. Heidegger and Sartre make of this 'call to others' a summons to be . . . (2001: 79)

For Heidegger, philosophy was '*authentic* living towards Being in history'; for Sartre, '*commitment* to being undeceived' (79). But does that mean, to return to an earlier question, that Existentialism is in itself confined solely to those who would call themselves, after Sartre, 'technicians and philosophers'?

It might seem rather too glib to counter that for Existentialism the commitment of any individual should be to existence, but for 'existence' as understood in the Existentialist sense this is perhaps as close to an answer as we can get, especially as formulated by Kierkegaard as 'the subjective thinker': 'To exist is an art. The subjective thinker is esthetic enough for his life to have esthetic content, ethical enough to regulate it, dialectical enough in thinking to master it. / The subjective thinker's task is to *understand himself in existence*' (1992: 351). It is not, then, in itself enough just to be a philosopher, or that one need be a philosopher in the first instance. In *The Trial* there is the suggestion that K. fails to exist in the Existential sense both before and after his arrest or awakening. Before the arrest he has an unthinking life, so this cannot be existence. After the arrest he is reluctant to take up responsibility for his life. This too is failing to exist. In both ways he is guilty. A Kierkegaardian reading would suggest that K. tries to substitute an absolute knowledge for the doubt that inevitably comes his way after the arrest. K. is sure of himself; an alternative system, equally sure of itself, begs to differ. However, K. then fails to take proper hold of the doubt that arises as the consequence of the collision between his own certainty and the certainty of the Law. He is accused of lacking 'interest' in his case, similar to Kierkegaard's accusation that those who assert objective knowledge over doubt fail to be 'interested'.

Existential thinkers therefore ask for a specific commitment to 'existence', where 'existence' is understood to be something that in itself is a commitment to 'exist' rather than just 'be'. Beyond that, they diverge, veering between commitment to others, politics, writing, language and philosophy.

If there is a current trend to be observed with respect to making Existentialism 'relevant' to today's concerns, it is probably most noticeable in the drive to see it in terms of an ethics it does or could provide: *French Existentialism: Consciousness, Ethics, and Relations with Others* (Giles, ed., 1999); *Heidegger and the Place of Ethics* (Lewis, 2005), which picks up on Heidegger's *existentiale* 'being-with' in *Being and Time*; 'Heidegger's Reading of Kierkegaard Revisited: From Ontological Abstraction to Ethical Concretion' (Huntington in Matuštík and Westphal, eds, 1995). If Kierkegaard is the founding father of Existential thought, then when Robert L. Perkins writes: 'Buber thought, and a lot of other people still do think, that Kierkegaard had little or no responsible understanding of the social and political aspects of existence' and sets out to disprove it (in Matuštík and Westphal, eds, 1995: 167), this would seem to confirm that Existential thought has consistently been seen as asocial or anti-social, and that any current interest can only operate by situating Existentialism predominantly within a contemporary ethical relevance. Bill Martin's *The Radical Project: Sartrean Investigations* (2000) indeed begins by asking if Sartre started his philosophical career with the intention of bringing about a 'just society' (2000: 1), as if this must be the first question we are to ask of Sartre. The possibility of a fully elaborated Existential ethics certainly continues to attract interesting work.

CHAPTER 12

AND NOW . . .?

It is a long time since any self-respecting philosopher would call him-or herself an Existentialist. Even in Existentialism's heyday, more thinkers refuted and refused the label 'Existentialist' than were willing to embrace it. Mary Warnock, writing at a time when Sartre had moved on to the Marxism espoused in *Critique of Dialectical Reason*, declared in her Introduction to *Being and Nothingness* that 'the time has come to consider existentialism as a part of the history of philosophy, not as a means of salvation nor as a doctrine of commitment' (Sartre, 1995: xviii). In a recent book on Kierkegaard, the editors note that one reason Kierkegaard may not have attracted the critical attention he deserves, at least in current critical theory, is that he has been too closely associated with Existentialism which 'is not the hottest ticket in town these days' (Matuštík and Westphal, eds, 1995: vii); in his Introduction to Sartre's *Critique of Dialectical Reason* Fredric Jameson consigns Existentialism to the past of intellectual history (Sartre, 2004a: xiii). Yet the afterglow of Existential thought thrives in numerous disciplinary fields, mainly with critics, commentators and researchers who aim to develop a particular aspect of Heidegger or Sartre. The work on phenomenology is wide, and since the late 1980s the study of consciousness has become extremely fashionable, a problem now worthy of effort rather than an irritating epiphenomenon, as noted at the end of Chapter 9.

One of the main problems for Existentialism is the perception that it is anti-social. The Introduction to *Kierkegaard in Post/Modernity* argues that all of the essays in the volume are concerned with a critical social project – in other words, Kierkegaard is commandeered in the name of the current critical and philosophical drive towards founding a communitarian ethic. It seems that the price to pay for a revived Existentialism would be to work out the ethics before the ontology. Work such as that promoting an 'Existential social theory' (Matuštík, 2002) would suggest that there is a way forward which takes into account poststructuralist developments after Existentialism's dominant period, but this would appear to be at the expense of Existentialism's core concepts of being, self and consciousness. The impetus here is to underwrite political freedom as an end in itself, at the same time as acknowledging the importance of the individual, but once again the argument really starts from its desired ethical end and endeavours to make the ontology fit. So although there is no discernible further development of Existential thought if we understand Existentialism to have being, self, and consciousness as its core concepts, as well as freedom, it is the case that for many, philosophers or not, Existentialism and the ideas that it holds and the concepts it addresses, continues to provide a way of thinking and existence which cannot be found elsewhere.

FURTHER READING

Existentialism
I would recommend *Existentialism: A Reconstruction* (second edition, 1999) by David E. Cooper as a recent, accessible book which also reviews Existentialism with respect to problems it finds central to philosophy as a whole, particularly the theme of alienation. The Introduction to *The Existentialist Reader: An Anthology of Key Texts* (Paul MacDonald, ed., 2000) provides an excellent summary of Existentialism, and this is enhanced by introductions to the interesting collection of complete pieces which comprise the book: Karl Jaspers, Gabriel Marcel, José Ortega y Gasset, Camus, Maurice Merleau-Ponty, Heidegger, de Beauvoir and Sartre. *Introducing Existentialism* (Appignanesi and Zarate, 2001) is worth reading, particularly for its engaged nature and the political perspective, although the reader should be warned that some foreknowledge of Existentialism is helpful, despite the title. I will always remain partial to John Macquarrie's *Existentialism* (1972/1991), since it was my first critical entry into the subject. There is still, of course, Sartre's *Existentialism and Humanism*, which provides a very lively engagement with Existentialism. More advanced, but a good book for tracing Existentialism through from Kierkegaard to the present, by way of those he influenced, is *Kierkegaard in Post/Modernity* (Matuštík and Westphal, eds, 1995). It has essays which devote themselves to Kierkegaard in relation to Sartre, Heidegger, Buber and Levinas, and to more recent critical theorists such as Habermas, Derrida, Kristeva and Gadamer. There are journals devoted to *Existential Analysis* (www.existentialanalysis.co.uk/), to Phenomenology and Existentialism (www.spep.org/index.html) and to Existentialism and Literature, *Stirrings Still*, available for free download via 'Lulu', (books.lulu.com/browse/). There are two websites devoted wholly to Existentialism: *The Existential Primer*: www.tameri.com/csw/exist/ and *The Realm of Existentialism*: www.dividingline.com

Beginning Philosophy
There are two on-line philosophy sites with substantial entries on all writers and themes germane to Existential philosophy (and beyond) which I would recommend: The Internet Encyclopaedia of Philosophy (http://www.iep.

utm.edu/) and the Stanford Encyclopaedia of Philosophy (http://plato.stanford.edu/contents.html). If it is an introduction to philosophy as a subject that you are looking for, then Nigel Warburton's *Philosophy: The Basics* (2004) is a good way in. For more advanced work see the suggestions below.

Kierkegaard
Although it is probably the story of Abraham as related in *Fear and Trembling* which is the most cited of Kierkegaard's works by Sartre, Camus, de Beauvoir *et al.*, the key text is undoubtedly *Concluding Unscientific Postscript to 'Philosophical Fragments'*. However, if this looks a little daunting to begin with, *Fear and Trembling* itself, or *The Sickness unto Death*, accompanied by a good introduction (for example, Alastair Hannay's in the Penguin Classics versions) would be a worthwhile start before launching into *Concluding Unscientific Postscript*. *The Concept of Anxiety* is probably the text which most influenced Heidegger.

Nietzsche
Thus Spoke Zarathustra is usually regarded as the major work, and the reader might attempt this first. It is considerably longer than his other works, and an alternative might be to go for *The Gay Science* or *Beyond Good and Evil* as the initial read.

Heidegger
'What is Metaphysics?' provides discussion of Being and nothingness and is a good, brief introduction to Heidegger's style of writing and thinking. The main work is *Being and Time*, which is a difficult book, and it might be an idea to have something like Stephen Mulhall's guide, *Heidegger and 'Being and Time'* (2005), alongside you.

Sartre
Although the status of *Existentialism and Humanism* as a work that properly expounds Sartre's views is open to debate, this is still a good place to start, both for Sartrean Existentialism and for Existentialism itself. *Nausea* also presents itself as an accessible work with clear Existential themes. The somewhat larger and formidable *Being and Nothingness* remains the 'bible' of Existentialism, of course, but this might usefully be preceded by reading *The Imaginary*, particularly the final section, which provides a neat bridge from the psychological grounding of Sartre's work on consciousness to his philosophical thought on the same. In addition, there is the *Roads to Freedom* trilogy (*The Age of Reason*, *The Reprieve* and *Iron in the Soul*), and plays such as *The Flies*, *No Exit* and *Dirty Hands* all have their place and make interesting reading.

Camus
The Outsider and *The Myth of Sisyphus* are the most immediately relevant works to Existentialism, but *The Rebel* is also worth reading. Aronson's book *Camus and Sartre. The Story of a Friendship and the Quarrel that*

Ended It (2004) has a lot of biographical material and relates the points of disagreement for both writers.

The *Cambridge Companion* series has volumes devoted to Kierkegaard, Nietzsche, Kafka, Heidegger and Sartre and offers good and varied essays on these writers.

Fiction

I can only offer a few possibilities in the space provided, but if you want to dive in chronologically, then I have no doubt that you should begin with Dostoevksy's *Crime and Punishment* (1866). If your appetite is whetted by that, I would also suggest *The Brother's Karamazov* (1880). Joseph Conrad's tale *Heart of Darkness* (1899/1902) has a character, Kurtz, who takes it upon himself to 'transvalue all values', and the tale is complicated by the (inner) narrator Marlow's ambivalent reaction to Imperialism. If Conrad appeals, then there are also *Victory* (1915) and *Nostromo* (1904), with ideas from Schopenhauer and Nietzsche informing the novels. I will mention again Charlotte Perkins Gilman's 'The Yellow Wallpaper' (1892), Kate Chopin's 'The Awakening' (1899) and Katherine Mansfield's 'Bliss' (1918). Likewise, I think that Virginia Woolf's *Mrs Dalloway* (1925) deserves attention, and Lessing's *The Golden Notebook* (1962) is an impressive foray into mental disintegration in the midst of personal and political commitment. Kafka's *The Trial* (1925) is a must, but also his short stories, such as 'In the Penal Colony' and 'A Fasting-Artist', and another novel, *The Castle* (1926). Ralph Ellison's *Invisible Man* is a masterpiece and should be read regardless! As well as Saul Bellow's *The Victim* (1947), discussed in this book, his first novel, *Dangling Man* (1944) has Existential themes. Milan Kundera's *The Unbearable Lightness of Being* (1984) has an overtly Existential dimension. 'Cult classics' on the periphery of Existential concern are Joseph Heller's *Catch 22* (1961), a seminal absurdist fiction, and Robert M. Pirsig's *Zen and the Art of Motorcycle Maintenance* (1974). Readers often find 'the Existential' in the work of Samuel Beckett, and he is discussed as a writer on the Existential cusp by Edith Kern in *Existential Thought and Fictional Technique*, but we are drifting away here. Of course, there are the works by Camus and Sartre, already mentioned, and de Beauvoir's *The Blood of Others* (1945). *The Existential Imagination* (Karl and Hamalian, eds, 1973) has an enterprising selection from European literature, starting with de Sade's 'Dialogue between a Priest and a Dying Man', which bears comparison with the meeting between Meursault and the priest in Camus's *The Outsider* as Meursault awaits execution.

Themes

The following books do not necessarily address Existential thought directly, but provide extensions of the themes discussed in this book in other directions. For phenomenology, the classic, standard text is Herbert Spiegelberg's *The Phenomenological Movement*, and there continues to be a lively interest directly in phenomenology – for example, the *Journal of the British Society for Phenomenology* and The Society for Phenomenological and Existential Philosophy (SPEP). There has been a lot of work on consciousness in recent years from the scientific community, and Susan Blackmore's *Consciousness: An Introduction* gives a good and entertaining overview, although it doesn't pick up on consciousness in the phenomenological or Existential arena. *The Brain and the Inner World: An Introduction to the Neuroscience of Subjective Experience* by Mark Solms and Oliver Turnbull is a good entry into an area of research whereby neuroscience investigates the mechanisms of our experience of consciousness (discussed briefly in this book at the end of Chapter 9). On God and nothingness there is Bede Rundle's *Why there is Something rather than Nothing*, which begins with the 'theist's attempt to account for the existence of the universe' (Rundle, 2005: 1), although again here is a book which does not consider work from Existential thought. For those interested in a broad picture of 'the self' there is *The Idea of the Self: Thought and Experience in Western Europe since the Seventeenth Century* by Jerrold Seigel (2005), and the work of Charles Taylor, sometimes seen as a continuation of Existential thought, e.g. *The Ethics of Authenticity* (1991) and *Sources of the Self* (1992). *Existential Perspectives on Human Issues* (van Deurzen and Arnold-Baker, eds, 2005), with its focus on person-centred counselling, ranges widely and intelligently. A different perspective on self in a 'post-self' world can be garnered from the collection of essays in *Identities: Race, Class, Gender and Nationality* (Alcoff and Mendieta, eds, 2003). There may as yet be interesting connections to be made between the work of Slavoj Žižek and Existentialism, although primarily his own concerns are with ethics, politics and Lacanian psychoanalysis.

These are only a few suggestions for further reading. There is always the possibility, of course, of returning to the many writers connected with the first flush of Existentialism that there has not been the space in this book to cover: Karl Jaspers, Ortega y Gasset, Miguel de Unamuno, Nikolai Berdyaev, Lev Chestov, Gabriel Marcel, Maurice Merleau-Ponty, Paul Tillich.

BIBLIOGRAPHY

Adorno, T. (1986), *The Jargon of Authenticity*. London: Routledge.

Alcoff, M. and Mendieta, E., eds (2003), *Identities: Race, Class, Gender a Nationality*. Oxford: Blackwell.

Appignanesi, R. and Zarate, O. (2001), *Introducing Existentialism*. Duxfor Cambridge: Icon Books.

Aronson, R. (2004), *Camus and Sartre: The Story of a Friendship and t Quarrel that Ended It*. Chicago, IL: University of Chicago Press.

Bedford, M. (1972), *Existentialism and Creativity*. New York: Philosophic Library.

Bellow, S. (1968), *Dangling Man*. Harmondsworth, Middlesex: Penguin.

Bellow, S. (1996), *The Victim*. London: Penguin.

Blackmore, S. (2002), *Consciousness: An Introduction*. London: Hodder Stoughton.

Buber, M. (1996), *I and Thou*. New York: Touchstone/Simon and Schust

Camus, A. (1981), *The Outsider*. Harmondsworth, Middlesex: Penguin.

Camus, A. (2000a), *The Myth of Sisyphus*. London: Penguin.

Camus, A. (2000b), *The Rebel*. London: Penguin.

Chopin, K. (1995), *'The Awakening' and Other Stories*. Hertfordshi Wordsworth.

Conrad, J. (1975), *Nostromo*. London: Pan.

Conrad, J. (1980), *Victory*. Harmondsworth, Middlesex: Penguin.

Conrad, J. (1989), *Heart of Darkness*. London: Penguin.

Cooper, D. E. (1999), *Existentialism: A Reconstruction*. Second editic Oxford: Blackwell.

Critical Inquiry (Winter 1989). Symposium on Heidegger and Nazism, 15

Danto, A. C. (1991), *Sartre*. London: Fontana Press.

Darwin, C. (1982), *On the Origin of Species*. Harmondsworth, Middles Penguin.

de Beauvoir, S. (1976), *The Blood of Others*. Harmondsworth, Middles Penguin.

de Beauvoir, S. (1996), *The Ethics of Ambiguity*. New York: Citadel Pres

de Beauvoir, S. (1997), *The Second Sex*. London: Vintage.

Dostoevsky, F. (1980), *Crime and Punishment*. Harmondsworth, Middles Penguin.

Dostoevsky, F. (2003), *The Brothers Karamazov*. London: Penguin.

Douglas, J. D. and Johnson, J. M., eds (1977), *Existential Sociology*. Cambridge: Cambridge University Press.

Earnshaw, S. (1995), 'Love and the Subject', in J. Dowson and S. Earnshaw (eds), *Postmodern Subjects/Postmodern Texts*. Amsterdam/Atlanta: Rodopi, pp. 57–70.

Ellison, R. (1979), *Invisible Man*. Harmondsworth, Middlesex: Penguin.

Giles, J., ed. (1999), *French Existentialism: Consciousness, Ethics, and Relations with Others*. Amsterdam/Atlanta: Rodopi.

Gilman, C. P. (1989), 'The Yellow Wallpaper', in *The Norton Anthology of American Literature*, Volume 2, third edition, pp. 649–60.

Grimsley, R. (1970), *Kierkegaard: A Biographical Introduction*. London: Studio Vista.

Groundhog Day (1993), film. Directed by Harold Ramis. Columbia Tristar, USA.

Habermas, J. (1989), 'Work and *Weltanschauung*: the Heidegger Controversy from a German perspective', *Critical Inquiry*, 15: 431–56.

Harding, M. (2005), 'Language', in E. van Deurzen and C. Arnold-Baker (eds), pp. 93–9.

Heidegger, M. (1982), *The Basic Problems of Phenomenology*. Bloomington, IN: Indiana University Press.

Heidegger, M. (1995), *Being and Time*. Oxford: Blackwell.

Heidegger, M. (2004), *Basic Writings*. Revised and expanded edition. London: Routledge.

Heller, J. (1973), *Catch 22*. London: Jonathan Cape.

Holy Bible. Revised Standard Edition (1965), London: Nelson.

Honderich, T. (2004), *On Consciousness*. Edinburgh: Edinburgh University Press.

Huntington, P. J. (1995), 'Heidegger's Reading of Kierkegaard Revisited: From Ontological Abstraction to Ethical Concretion', in M. J. Matuštík and M. Westphal (eds), pp. 43–65.

Husserl, E. (1969), *Ideas: General Introduction to Pure Phenomenology*. London: George Allen & Unwin.

Journal of the British Society for Phenomenology. Department of Politics and Philosophy, Manchester Metropolitan University.

Kafka, F. (1973), *The Castle*. London: Secker & Warburg.

Kafka, F. (1978), *The Trial*. Harmondsworth, Middlesex: Penguin.

Kafka, F. (2002), *Franz Kafka: Stories 1904–1924*. London: Abacus.

Karl, F. R. and Hamalian, L., eds (1973), *The Existential Imagination: From de Sade to Sartre*. London: Picador.

Kaufmann, W. (1975), *Existentialism: From Dostoevsky to Sartre*. Revised and expanded edition. New York: The New American Library.

Kellner, G. F. (1958), *Existentialism and Education*. New York: John Wiley.

Kern, E. (1970), *Existential Thought and Fictional Technique*. New Haven, CT: Yale University Press.

Kierkegaard, S. (1942), *Repetition*. Princeton, NJ: Princeton University Press.

Kierkegaard, S. (1959), *Either/Or*. Volume II. New York: Anchor Books.

Kierkegaard, S. (1980), *The Concept of Anxiety*. Princeton, NJ: Princeton University Press.

Kierkegaard, S. (1985), *Philosophical Fragments*. Princeton, NJ: Princeton University Press.

Kierkegaard, S. (1988), *Stages on Life's Way*. Princeton, NJ: Princeton University Press.

Kierkegaard, S. (1992), *Concluding Unscientific Postscript to 'Philosophical Fragments'*. Volume 1. Princeton, NJ: Princeton University Press.

Kierkegaard, S. (2003), *Fear and Trembling*. London: Penguin.

Kierkegaard, S. (2004a), *Either/Or* (abridged). London: Penguin.

Kierkegaard, S. (2004b), *The Sickness unto Death*. London: Penguin.

Kundera, M. (1984), *The Unbearable Lightness of Being*. London: Faber.

Laing, R. D. (1983), *The Divided Self*. Harmondsworth, Middlesex: Penguin.

Lavrin, J. (1971), *Nietzsche: A Biographical Introduction*. London: Studio Vista.

Lessing, D. (1989), *The Golden Notebook*. London: Grafton.

Levinas, E. (1996), *Totality and Infinity*. Pittsburgh, PA: Duquesne University Press.

Lewis, M. (2005), *Heidegger and the Place of Ethics*. New York: Continuum.

Lodge, D. (2002), *Consciousness and the Novel*. London: Secker and Warburg.

MacDonald, P. S., ed. (2000), *The Existentialist Reader: An Anthology of Key Texts*. Edinburgh: Edinburgh University Press.

Macquarrie, J. (1972), *Existentialism*. Harmondsworth, Middlesex: Penguin.

Macquarrie, J. (1980), *An Existentialist Theology. A Comparison of Heidegger and Bultmann*. Harmondsworth, Middlesex: Penguin.

Mansfield, K. (2002), *Selected Stories*. Oxford: Oxford University Press.

Martin, B. (2000), *The Radical Project: Sartrean Investigations*. Lanham, MD: Rowman & Littlefield Publishers.

Matuštík, M. J. and Westphal, M., eds (1995), *Kierkegaard in Post/Modernity*. Bloomington, IN: Indiana University Press.

Matuštík, M. B. (2002), 'Existential social theory after the poststructuralist and communication turns', *Human Studies*, 25: 147–64.

Merleau-Ponty, M. (2002), *Phenomenology of Perception*. London: Routledge.

Mulhall, S. (2005), *Heidegger and 'Being and Time'*. Oxon: Routledge.

Nietzsche, F. (1974), *The Gay Science with a Prelude in Rhymes and an Appendix of Songs*. New York: Vintage Books.

Nietzsche, F. (1979), *'Twilight of the Idols' and 'The Anti-Christ'*. Harmondsworth, Middlesex: Penguin.

Nietzsche, F. (1981), *Thus Spoke Zarathustra*. Harmondsworth, Middlesex: Penguin.

Nietzsche, F. (1983), *Ecce Homo*. Harmondsworth, Middlesex: Penguin.

Nietzsche, F. (2000), *Basic Writings of Nietzsche*. New York: Random House.

Nietzsche, F. (2003), *Beyond Good and Evil*. London: Penguin.

Perkins, R. L., 'The Politics of Existence: Buber and Kierkegaard', in M. J. Matuštík and M. Westphal (eds), pp. 167–81.

Peters, H. (1991), *The Existential Woman*. New York: Peter Lang.

Plato (1983), *The Symposium*. Harmondsworth, Middlesex: Penguin.

Pirsig, R. M. (1989), *Zen and the Art of Motorcycle Maintenance*. London: Vintage.

Roberts, D. E. (1957), *Existentialism and Religious Belief*. New York, Oxford University Press.

Rundle, B. (2005), *Why there is Something rather than Nothing*. Oxford: Clarendon Press.

Salinger, J. D. (1986), *The Catcher in the Rye*. Harmondsworth: Middlesex.

Sartre, J.-P. (1964), *Words*. London: Hamish Hamilton.

Sartre, J.-P. (1968), *Search for a Method*. New York: Vintage Books.

Sartre, J.-P. (1970), *The Reprieve*. Harmondsworth, Middlesex: Penguin.

Sartre, J.-P. (1973), *Existentialism and Humanism*, London: Eyre Methuen.

Sartre, J.-P. (1979), *Nausea*. Harmondsworth, Middlesex: Penguin.

Sartre, J.-P. (1981), *Three Plays ('Altona'; 'Men Without Shadows'; 'The Flies')*. Harmondsworth, Middlesex: Penguin.

Sartre, J.-P. (1989), *No Exit and Three Other Plays*. New York: Vintage International.

Sartre, J.-P. (1995), *Being and Nothingness*. London: Routledge.

Sartre, J.-P. (2001), *The Age of Reason*. London: Penguin.

Sartre, J.-P. (2002), *Iron in the Soul*. London: Penguin.

Sartre, J.-P. (2004a), *Critique of Dialectical Reason. Volume One*. London: Verso.

Sartre, J.-P. (2004b), *The Imaginary*. London: Routledge.

Sartre, J.-P. (2004c), *Sketch for a Theory of the Emotions*. London: Routledge.

Sartre, J.-P. (2004d), *The Transcendence of the Ego*. London: Routledge.

Sartre, J.-P. (2004e), *What is Literature?* London: Routledge.

Seigel, J. (2005), *The Idea of the Self: Thought and Experience in Western Europe since the Seventeenth Century*. Cambridge: Cambridge University Press.

Shaw, R. (2003), 'Teaching "The Yellow Wallpaper" and Existentialism in the Classroom', in J. A Weinstock, ed., *The Pedagogical Wallpaper: Teaching Charlotte Perkins Gilman's "The Yellow Wallpaper"*. New York: Peter Lang, pp. 64–81.

Simons, J., ed. (2002), *From Kant to Lévi-Strauss: The Background to Contemporary Critical Theory*. Edinburgh: Edinburgh University Press.

Solms, M. and Turnbull, O. (2002), *The Brain and the Inner World: An Introduction to the Neuroscience of Subjective Experience*. New York: Other Press.

Spiegelberg, H. (1984), *The Phenomenological Movement*. Third revised and enlarged edition. The Hague: Martinus Nijhoff Publishers.

Steiner, G. (1978), *Heidegger*. Glasgow: Fontana.

Steiner, G. (2004), 'Drawn from Silence', Review of *Paul Celan et Martin Heidegger* (Hadrien France-Lanord), *Times Literary Supplement*, 1 October 2004.

Stirrings Still: The International Journal of Existential Literature. Published by Binghamton University, New York.

Taylor, C. (1991), *The Ethics of Authenticity*. Cambridge, MA: Harvard University Press.

Taylor, C. (1992), *Sources of the Self*. Cambridge: Cambridge University Press.

van Deurzen, E. and Arnold-Baker, C., eds (2005), *Existential Perspectives on Human Issues*. Basingstoke, Hampshire: Palgrave Macmillan.

Wahl, J. (1969), *Philosophies of Existence: An Introduction to the Basic Thought of Kierkegaard, Heidegger, Jaspers, Marcel, Sartre*. London: Routledge.

Warburton, N. (2004), *Philosophy: The Basics*. London: Routledge.

Warnock, M. (1970), *Existentialism*. Oxford: Oxford University Press.

Wilson, C. (1963), *The Outsider*. London: Pan.

Woolf, V. (1976), *Mrs Dalloway*. London: Triad.

Yalom, I. D. (1980), *Existential Psychotherapy*. New York: Basic Books.

Žižek, S. and Daly, G. (2004), *Conversations with Žižek*. Cambridge: Polity.

INDEX

abandonment 141–2, 150
Abraham (biblical) 17, 26, 27, **34–5**, 44,
  52, 54, 103, 151, 158, 159, 160
absurd, the 8, 13, 18, 19, 26, 40, 41,
  94–5, 97–105, 119, 124, 126,
  161
'act, to' (as in agency) 12, 39, 88, 92–3,
  105, 111–12, 120, 154, 161, 164,
  166, 169
'actual existing individual' **36–7**, 43, 44,
  73
aesthetic life/stage (Kierkegaard) 16,
  31, **32–3**, 39, 57, 113, 163–4
aesthetics 9–12, 39
alienation 5, 8, 11, 20, 31, 37, 65, 95,
  119, 145
ambiguity **161–2**, 164
amor fati ('love of [one's] fate') 55
angst 8, 15, 16, 31, 124 *see also*
  'anxiety'
anguish *see 'anxiety'*
animals 20–1, 42, 47, 59
anti-psychiatry 9
anxiety 3, 4, 8, 11, 15, 16–17, 21, 26,
  31, 41, 47, 65, 68, 71, 73, 75, 76, 77,
  83–4, 95, 96, 101, 124, 134, **146–7**,
  162
Appignanesi, Richard 13, 21, 23, 167
'appropriation' 31, 38
Arendt, Hannah 13
Arnold-Baker, C. 9
Aronson, R. 127
art 10, 100
atheism 5, 17, 141–2, 143–5, 149
atheist existentialism 101, 142, 143,
  151, 164
authenticity 3, 4, 12, 13, 14, 15, 18, 24,

31, 55–6, 57, 59, 64, 67, 68–9, 70,
  88, 103, 111, 114, 115, 116–18, 119,
  120, 122–3, 124, 125, 134, 145–6,
  157, 160, 164, 165, 167 *see also*
  'inauthenticity'
authorship 42–3, 46
averageness 117
'awakening' 11, **14–17**, 18, 32, 96, 99,
  145, 150, 151, 165, 167

'bad faith' 8, 18, 75, 78, **84–5**, 92, 155,
  164
Beats, the 9
'becoming' 31, **37–8**, 39
being/Being (see 27 n.1) 2, 7, 8, 12, 20,
  21, 22, 23, 24, 25, **27 n.1**, 31, 38, 44,
  59–70, 73, 77, **81–90**, 95, 99, 103,
  111–12, **113–26**, 127, 129–31, 133,
  134, 135, 137, 142, 146, 147, 150,
  156, 157, 158, 164, 165, 167, 168,
  170
being-for-others 87, 165
Being-in-the-world 23, **62**, 65, 67, 146,
  164
being-in-the-world-with-Others 14,
  62–3, 86–7, 164, 165
'being-there' *see 'Dasein'*
being-with 168
Bellow, Saul 165–6
Berkeley, George 22, 129
birth 65, 70
Blackmore, Susan 139
body, the 17, 23, 24, 47, 56–8,
  135–7
'bracketing' 15, 90–1, 128, 129, 131,
  132–3
Blake, William 9